Psych 2.0

ONLINE EXPERIENCE GUI

TAMARA RAHHAL

University of Massachusetts–Amherst

MATTHEW SCHULKIND

Amherst College

 Higher Education

Boston   Burr Ridge, IL   Dubuque, IA   New York   San Francisco   St. Louis
Bangkok   Bogotá   Caracas   Kuala Lumpur   Lisbon   London   Madrid   Mexico City
Milan   Montreal   New Delhi   Santiago   Seoul   Singapore   Sydney   Taipei   Toronto

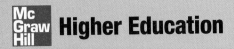
Higher Education

1 2 3 4 5 6 7 8 9 0 (DOC)/(DOC) 0 9 8

ISBN: 978-0-07-726440-6
MHID: 0-07-726440-1

Editor in Chief: *Michael Ryan*
Director, Editorial: *Beth Mejia*
Sponsoring Editor: *Mike Sugarman*
Marketing Manager: *James Headley*
Director of Development: *Dawn Groundwater*
Developmental Editor: *Emily Pecora*
Production Editor: *David Blatty*
Manuscript Editor: *Andrea McCarrick*
Design Manager: *Cassandra Chu*
Text and Cover Designer: *Maureen McCutcheon*
Production Supervisor: *Louis Swaim*
Composition: *Laserwords*
Printing: *45# New Era Matte Plus, R. R. Donnelley*

Cover and interior image: *istockpthoto © Ann Marie Kurtz*

Library of Congress Cataloging-in-Publication Data

Rahhal, Tamara.
  Psych 2.0 online experience guide / Tamara Rahhal, Matthew Schulkind.—1st ed.
    p. cm.
  ISBN-13: 978-0-07-726440-6 (alk. paper)
  ISBN-10: 0-07-726440-1 (alk. paper)
  1. Psychology—Textbooks. 2. Psychology—Study and teaching. I. Schulkind, Matthew. II. Title.
  BF121.R27 2009
  150.78—dc22   2008019580

www.mhhe.com

Psych 2.0 . . . it's what you need.

TO THE INSTRUCTOR

Are you looking for a solution for traditional, hybrid, or online courses? Are you searching for a set of engaging conceptually based activities to reinforce the foundational ideas in your lectures and reading assignments? Do you want to integrate or upgrade a lab, recitation section, or new course activities? If you answered yes to one or more of these questions, *Psych 2.0* is for you.

- Constructed as an enhanced course cartridge sold in conjunction with this printed guidebook, *Psych 2.0* can be easily added to your syllabus or online course whether you use Blackboard or a number of other LMS platforms.

- Easy to assign and integrate into any course format, *Psych 2.0*'s engaging companion textbook helps students work purposefully and successfully with the online tutorials.

- Affordable and fairly priced, *Psych 2.0* is available at the same low price to all students, regardless of whether they purchase a new or a used textbook.

- Based on extensive research on the general psychology concepts that students most need to master, *Psych 2.0* helps students get the key points they need while conveying the variety, breadth, and relevance of the field.

Content Based on Contextual Research

Over the past three years, McGraw-Hill has engaged in extensive ethnographic research on college campuses—in classrooms, dormitories, learning centers, and conference rooms. The foundation for this research agenda is an innovative program called "We Listen." The "We Listen" project involved hundreds of McGraw-Hill employees representing sales, marketing, management, and product development sitting in on 1,000 hours of introductory psychology classes. We watched, listened, and learned not only about the action potential, correlation not equaling causation, and the fundamental attribution error, but also about what tools instructors use and don't use, how you use them (or not), how much time you spend on core concepts, which concepts are toughest to teach and to learn, and when students "light up" and when they "zone out." We are hard at work to apply all we've learned in the development of new, extraordinarily useful products for teaching and learning.

Psych 2.0 is innovative in its focus on core concepts, in its marriage of traditional (print) and new (digital), and in its concerted effort to bring online resources into the mainstream of college courses.

Core Concepts *Psych 2.0* is divided into fifteen general topic areas roughly corresponding to a fifteen-week term or to a typical introductory psychology textbook's table of contents. Within each topic area are interactive activities that explicitly aim to help students master the fundamental ideas of psychology. From learning the steps of the scientific method to using classical conditioning to sell surfboard wax, from developing your working memory by serving tables at Café Cogito to answering a series of questions that demonstrates the fundamental attribution error at work on a personal level, students that interact with *Psych 2.0* will be engaged: laughing, questioning, and trying again. When they click "*Exit,*" they take with them a more dynamic understanding of the discipline.

Psych 2.0 is an innovative combination of print and online resources. The Web site at http://www.mhhe.com/psych2 consists of interactive activities on core psychological concepts, plus instructional tools to help you integrate the content in your course and to assess students on what they learn.

The printed guide, *Psych 2.0: Online Experience Guide,* is written by Tamara Rahhal of the University of Massachusetts–Amherst and Matthew Schulkind of Amherst College. It contains introductions that place each activity in a meaningful context for learning, plus tips to guide students in successfully completing each activity. Each *Guide* contains a passcode that provides access to the Web-based content.

Integrating *Psych 2.0* into Your Course

Extensive research on how instructors are using technology in teaching told us that you need materials that make it easier to seamlessly incorporate online materials into your course. The *Psych 2.0* instructor resource site provides all you need to implement this innovative course resource.

As an instructor, you have access to all of the content on the student site. In addition, the instructor site offers Lecture Links for your personal PowerPoints, and EZ Test assessment questions associated with each activity. All of *Psych 2.0* can be used in its existing form or delivered via course cartridge to seamlessly integrate with your existing course Web site.

Lecture Links are small portions of each activity that you can embed in your lecture PowerPoints to introduce the activity to your students. Setting up the activity in this way helps reinforce the importance of the assignment and primes students for what they'll encounter online. Lecture Links are in the form of one or two PowerPoint slides or a small executable file that enables you to show the online content even if you don't have Internet access in the classroom.

Ten Assessment Questions are provided for each activity, in both Word format and embedded in EZ Test, McGraw-Hill's testing engine. **EZ Test** is a flexible and easy-to-use electronic testing program. Using EZ Test, assessment questions based on *Psych 2.0* content can be integrated into existing quizzes and exams. Multiple versions of the test can be created, and any test can be exported for use with course-management systems such as WebCT, Blackboard, or PageOut. **EZ Test Online** is a new service that gives you a place to easily administer your EZ Test–created exams and quizzes online. The program is available for Windows and Macintosh environments.

Registration/Log-in Information

The instructor site is password protected. Please contact your McGraw-Hill campus sales representative to receive a username and password. If you do not know who your sales representative is, please use our Rep Locator at http://www.mhhe.com/rep. Do not attempt to register using a student registration code. You will not have access to the Instructor Edition.

T O   T H E   S T U D E N T

We urge you to make the most of this resource. It has been designed by psychology instructors and instructional designers to capture the essence of core psychological concepts—those that you need to master to do well in this course. Incidentally, many of these concepts have direct relevance in your everyday life as well. From being a more critical consumer of information purveyed by the media to understanding the different motivations underlying human interactions, *Psych 2.0*—and your psychology course—can help you see the world in an exciting new way.

As a server and manager at Café Cogito, you build on psychological principles to be successful.

Attend a Star Trek convention, and use your understanding of psychology to determine if Harry, Jill, and Marcus are *really* Klingons.

Use concepts of classical conditioning to develop a winning ad campaign for Wax-Trax surfboard wax.

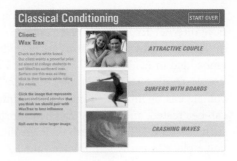

ACKNOWLEDGMENTS

Thank you to the following individuals who have creatively and tenaciously helped to guide the development of content for *Psych 2.0*. Their insights have resulted in learning activities that draw directly from their many years, of experience teaching introductory psychology students.

Melissa Acevedo, Westchester Community College, New York
Dr. Acevedo's research interests focus on the effects of social projection on cooperative behavior in social dilemmas. She uses technology, such as classroom response systems and PsychInteractive, to enhance student motivation and performance in her classroom.

Jeff Green, Virginia Commonwealth University
Dr. Green's research revolves around self-concept, investigating how people protect the self via selective memory and studying how affective states such as sadness and anger influence self-conceptions. "I like the potential of new technology to engage students by asking them to think deeply about and apply new knowledge. Interactive technologies improve both motivation and understanding and are therefore an indispensable tool for instructors."

Julie Bauer Morrison, Glendale Community College, Arizona
Dr. Morrison is a cognitive psychologist with research interests in the ways that technology can improve learning. As her primary area of research investigates the use of graphics and animation, she is particularly interested in the PsychInteractive project. "One of the joys of teaching introductory psychology for me is watching students realize that psychology is a science that reveals all aspects of our behavior and mental processes. PsychInteractive is a hands-on way of exposing students to the material in a way that increases the likelihood they will integrate it into their own lives."

Phil Pegg, Western Kentucky University
Dr. Pegg is a doctor in clinical psychology with an emphasis on adult psychopathology and behavioral medicine. He characterizes his research interests as "eclectic, covering the gamut from behavioral medicine to personality theory."

Tanya Renner, Kapi'olani Community College, Hawaii

Dr. Renner's interest in the use of technology for introductory psychology is based on her continuing efforts to create opportunities for students to learn experientially, apply psychological concepts to real-life situations, and think critically about psychological concepts. She regularly uses the Interactivities found on PsychInteractive in her class and values the ways that they address elements of critical thinking, such as taking another's perspective, evaluating evidence for relevance, and determining what kind of evidence is needed to answer a question or solve a problem.

Carla G. Strassle, York College of Pennsylvania

Dr. Strassle is a clinical psychologist with research interests in assessment and treatment effectiveness. She considers introductory psychology the first chance to help students understand how fascinating, diverse, and thought-provoking psychology can be. She says, "Nothing beats covering a topic and having students gain new insight that helps them see the world in a different way. This truly is a gateway class to the rest of this field."

Jim Stringham, University of Georgia

Dr. Stringham has taught psychology courses for seven years and specializes in sensation and perception. Although he has found that many faculty members do not enjoy teaching introductory psychology, it is one his favorite courses to teach. "It is basically a 'greatest hits' of psychology! I believe that a professor's enthusiasm for a subject is crucial to students' interest in the material; to this end, I do my best to convey my enthusiasm for psychology." Dr. Stringham's research interests include color vision, the effects of diet on vision, and macular degeneration.

Thank you also to the following instructors who provided detailed feedback on the Psych 2.0 guidebook content and site structure:

> Mike Enders, Northcentral Technical College
> Lauretta Reeves, the University of Texas at Austin
> John Wright, Washington State University

CONTENTS

Psychological Perspectives

1.1 Multiple Causes of Behavior

The simplest definition of psychology is that it is the study of behavior. The goal of most psychologists is not to predict behavior but rather to understand the underlying causes of behavior. For example, you are about to watch a video in which a woman named Amber explains her decision to drop out of college. One might ask what Amber will do now that she has dropped out, but most psychologists would be more interested in trying to understand what factors led to her decision to leave college.

The simplest goal of this video is to demonstrate that identifying the factors that cause any particular behavior is difficult. Often, multiple factors seem to play a role, and it is difficult to know which of these are responsible for a specific action. Of course, you do not need the video to teach you this. You have probably been puzzled at times by the actions of your parents or friends and have tried—in vain—to understand why these people chose to do what they did.

Psychologists try to simplify the problem of understanding behavior by focusing on a subset of potential explanations. Thus, the most important goal of this video is to familiarize you with the kinds of motivations that are studied by the different branches of psychology. *Social psychologists,* for example, tend to examine how the actions and attitudes of other people influence behavior. *Biological psychologists* tend to look for physiological explanations for behavior. *Cognitive psychologists* examine how intellectual functions like memory and intelligence influence behavior. *Clinical psychologists* examine how various forms of psychological disease affect behavior. You should also be aware that many psychologists study issues that cross these boundaries (e.g., the biological causes of psychological disease).

TIPS

- As you watch the video, keep track of which explanations you think most likely explain Amber's decision.

- Try to categorize the potential explanations according to the branches of psychology that you think would be most interested in investigating each cause for Amber's behavior.

- Decide whether the factors that you think are most important all fall within the same branch or more than one branch of psychology.

Please watch this video carefully and try to understand the factors that caused Amber to drop out of college. On the next page, we will ask you several questions about her behavior.

REFLECTION QUESTION

Leslie, a 20-year-old woman, decided to join the armed forces. List as many reasons as you can think of to explain Leslie's behavior. (Remember that there are no right or wrong answers; just try to generate a lot of reasons.) Now go back to your list of reasons, and try to place each of them within a particular area of psychology (e.g. biological, cognitive, clinical, developmental). Do you find that many of your reasons group together within one causal area, or are they evenly distributed among a variety of causes?

MULTIPLE-CHOICE ITEMS

Trevor, an 11–year-old boy, is doing poorly in school. He visits the school counselor, who learns about many possible influences on his academic behavior. Trevor has been feeling depressed lately because his friends have begun to ignore him on the playground. The kids tease Trevor because he isn't maturing as fast physically as many of the other boys. Trevor has not been sleeping well because he is always worrying about what other people think about him. Trevor's parents try to encourage him by giving him money when he receives good grades. However, they also punish him by taking away money when he does poorly. Trevor tries to study hard, but he often has trouble understanding the material his teachers give him.

1. Which type of psychologist would be *most* interested in Trevor's physical growth concerns?
   a. social psychologist
   b. abnormal psychologist
   c. developmental psychologist
   d. learning psychologist

2. A psychologist interested in abnormal psychology would be *most* interested in which part of Trevor's issues?
   a. Trevor's depressed mood
   b. Trevor's difficulty with the school material
   c. Trevor's parents' attempts at rewarding his behavior
   d. Trevor's teasing from his friends

3. Someone from the social-psychology perspective would be *least* interested in

   a. Trevor's growth patterns.
   b. Trevor's relationship with his parents.
   c. Trevor's interactions with his peers.
   d. Trevor's discussions with his teachers.

4. The school counselor is trained in examining how "patterns of consciousness" affect people's behaviors. The school counselor would most likely question Trevor more about his

   a. parents.   b. study habits.   c. growth patterns.   d. sleep habits.

1.2 Five Perspectives in Psychology

Although psychologists are united by their interest in understanding behavior, the field can be split into five different perspectives:

1. Neuroscience
2. Behavioral psychology
3. Cognitive psychology
4. Humanistic psychology
5. Psychodynamic psychology

These five perspectives focus on different factors that shape behavior. Some perspectives suggest that behavior can be explained in terms of internal causes like biology or personality. Others look to external causes like the environment or past experience. Some perspectives emphasize that people have free will: the ability to control their behavior and destiny. Other perspectives are deterministic: they suggest that free will is an illusion and that our behavior is constrained by a variety of factors beyond our control.

The video portion of this activity explains the different perspectives and outlines what kinds of factors are the primary determinants of human behavior. The quiz that follows the video was designed to provide you with some feedback about which branch of psychology is a good fit for your current attitudes about the different perspectives. The extent to which you agree or disagree with these statements will likely change as you learn more about psychology, so it would be a good idea to keep these issues in mind as you move through the term.

TIPS

- As you listen to the video explanations, think about the different theoretical views that underlie each perspective. Which ones emphasize free will? Which ones are more deterministic? Which of the perspectives look to explain behavior in terms of internal causes? Which ones are primarily concerned with external causes?

- After completing the quiz, jot down which of the five perspectives are most and least compatible with your current views. Write this information into the front cover of your notebook. At the end of the semester, you can revisit your notes to see how much your attitudes have changed as a result of taking this course.

To learn more about a psychological perspective, roll your mouse over each picture for a summary of that perspective's approach. You can also click on a picture to view a video that explains a particular perspective.

Neuroscience   Behavioral   Cognitive   Humanistic   Psychodynamic

< Back   Next >

REFLECTION QUESTION

Jason meets Alina in a bar and is immediately attracted to her. How might each of the five perspectives in psychology (neuroscience and behavioral, cognitive, humanistic, and psychodynamic psychology) explain Jason's attraction to Alina?

MULTIPLE-CHOICE ITEMS

1. Clyde's father has suffered several episodes of depression over his lifetime. Clyde wonders if his father's depressions might have been triggered by a neurotransmitter deficiency. To answer his questions, Clyde would likely visit a(n)
   a. neuroscientist.   c. humanist.
   b. behaviorist.   d. cognitive psychologist.

2. Jennie believes that she is in control of her own life and can achieve whatever goals she sets for herself. Jennie's beliefs are in line with which perspective in psychology?
   a. cognitive   c. behavioral
   b. humanistic   d. psychodynamic

3. _____ examine the differences between automatic and controlled processes in thinking.
   a. Neuropsychologists   c. Humanistic psychologists
   b. Behavioral psychologists   d. Cognitive psychologists

4. Dr. Watson observes how children react to receiving a prize for doing well on a math test. Dr. Watson is most likely a _____ psychologist.
   a. cognitive   c. behavioral
   b. psychodynamic   d. humanistic

5. Jennifer is always forgetting to call her mother. Although Jennifer cannot pinpoint why this happens, a _____ would wonder if Jennifer was forgetting due to unconscious forces.
   a. behavioral psychologist   c. humanistic psychologist
   b. psychodynamic psychologist   d. neuropsychologist

1.3 Subfields and Careers

If you ask people what kind of work psychologists do, most will answer that psychologists provide counseling to depressed or otherwise emotionally disturbed individuals. Although many psychologists do serve as counselors, the kinds of psychologists and the kinds of work that they do are extraordinarily varied. Some work in laboratories performing complex neurochemical experiments that you might associate with biochemistry. Some work in offices designing advertising campaigns aimed at convincing consumers to purchase a particular product. Others consult with law-enforcement officials and lawyers about how best to interview crime witnesses. Some work—literally—in the field, observing the behavior of birds or primates to learn something about their social structure and cognitive abilities. As the brochure (online at http://www.apa.org/topics/psychologycareer.html) published by the American Psychological Association (APA) will make clear, the number of paths you can follow and the different kinds of work you can pursue are virtually without limit.

TIPS

- This is a very long, thorough document. For now, take time to read the first two sections, which give an overview of the kinds of work done by professionals in the field.

- Save this document for future reference. If you elect to major in psychology, the information throughout this guide may help you select courses that will lead you to an appealing career after college.

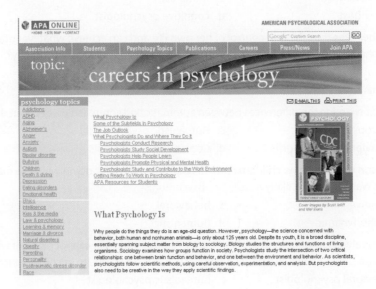

REFLECTION QUESTION

Although psychologists are hard at work in a variety of professional settings, some controversy surrounds the work of psychologists in certain fields. In particular, some psychologists are critical of their peers who testify in legal cases or serve the intelligence and military communities. What ethical questions might be raised about psychologists serving in these capacities? Are there ways to ensure that psychological science is used responsibly or even constructively in serving these areas?

MULTIPLE-CHOICE ITEMS

1. In which of the following settings would you be likely to find a psychologist at work?
   a. at a local public school
   b. at a criminal court hearing
   c. in the offices of a large corporation
   d. All of the above

2. Dr. Logan is a psychologist who studies memory. He would most likely be a
   a. clinical psychologist.
   b. cognitive psychologist.
   c. industrial/organizational psychologist.
   d. social psychologist.

3. Neuropsychologists tend to
   a. focus on research rather than treatment/practice.
   b. focus on treatment/practice rather than research.
   c. focus on both treatment/practice and research.
   d. ignore both treatment/practice and research.

4. An airplane manufacturer wants to ensure that the cockpit of a newly developed jet is "pilot friendly"; that is, the displays and controls are placed so that the pilot can easily see and use them to fly the plane. The company should be looking to hire a
   a. human factors psychologist.
   b. evolutionary psychologist.
   c. forensic psychologist.
   d. None of the above

5. As a field, psychology tends to study questions at the intersection of
   a. biology and sociology.
   b. brain function and behavior.
   c. brain function and sociology.
   d. sociology and behavior.

CHAPTER TWO

Science and Methodology

2.1 The Scientific Method

Just like research in physics or chemistry, research in psychology is guided by the principles of the scientific method. An observation is made about a behavior of interest. A hypothetical explanation is proposed. Then an experiment is conducted to determine whether the hypothetical explanation is valid or not. For example, a psychologist might notice that adolescents who engage in violent behavior often report that they play violent video games. This might lead to the following hypothesis: violent video games cause violent behavior. An experiment could be conducted in which one group of subjects (the experimental group) plays violent video games, while another group (the control group) plays nonviolent games. The subjects could then complete a questionnaire probing for violent versus nonviolent solutions to hypothetical conflicts. In this example, the kind of video game would be the independent variable, and the responses on the questionnaire would be the dependent variable. If the experimental group tended to show more violent responses on a subsequent questionnaire, we would conclude that the hypothesis was valid: violent video games do promote violent behavior. Otherwise we might conclude that the hypothesis was invalid: violent video games do not promote violent behavior.

In this activity, you will have the opportunity to complete three stages of the scientific method.

Observation: you will watch a group of circles moving against a colored background.

Hypothesis: you will generate hypotheses regarding the movement of the balls; for example, when two orange balls collide, they fuse into one ball.

Experiment: you will create a control group and an experimental group to test your hypothesis.

TIPS

- The behavior of the balls is not random. Collisions between two kinds of balls always produce the same effect.

- The color of the background is an important variable to consider—collisions have different effects depending on the color of the background. So your hypothesis should include background color as the independent variable. For example, when two orange balls collide *on a white background,* they fuse into one ball.

- Be sure to generate two or three different hypotheses before moving forward to the experimental portion of the activity; otherwise you might have difficulty selecting a hypothesis to test.

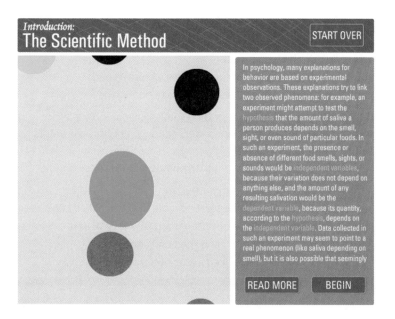

In psychology, many explanations for behavior are based on experimental observations. These explanations try to link two observed phenomena: for example, an experiment might attempt to test the hypothesis that the amount of saliva a person produces depends on the smell, sight, or even sound of particular foods. In such an experiment, the presence or absence of different food smells, sights, or sounds would be independent variables, because their variation does not depend on anything else, and the amount of any resulting salivation would be the dependent variable, because its quantity, according to the hypothesis, depends on the independent variable. Data collected in such an experiment may seem to point to a real phenomenon (like saliva depending on smell), but it is also possible that seemingly

READ MORE   BEGIN

REFLECTION QUESTIONS

1. Generate your own hypothesis about differences in how and what males and females order in restaurants.

2. How could you set up an experiment to test your hypothesis? Be sure to include independent and dependent variables.

MULTIPLE-CHOICE ITEMS

Professor Boredom has noticed that his students keep falling asleep during his lectures. He thinks that keeping the lights in the lecture hall at their brightest level will help keep students awake. He decides to give the same lecture to three groups of people. He holds one class session with bright lights, one class session with normal lighting, and one class session with dim lights. Professor Boredom has a teaching assistant count the number of sleepers at the end of each class.

1. What is Professor Boredom's hypothesis in this example?
   a. Bright lights will keep more students awake in class than dimmer lights.
   b. Lighting will have no effect on students' wakefulness.
   c. Sleepy students prefer dimmer lights during class time than alert students.
   d. Alert students prefer dimmer lights during class time than sleepy students.

2. The independent variable in the above experiment is
   a. the number of sleeping students.
   b. the level of light in the lecture hall.
   c. the students' performance on a quiz covering the lecture material.
   d. the number of pages of notes the students take during the lecture.

3. The dependent variable in the above experiment is
   a. the number of sleeping students.
   b. the level of light in the lecture hall.
   c. students' performance on a quiz covering the lecture material.
   d. the number of pages of notes the students take during the lecture.

4. After reading about research demonstrating that regular aerobic exercise improves a person's memory performance, Olga wonders if lifting weights daily would have the same effect. Olga has generated a(n)
   a. theory.　　b. construct.　　c. hypothesis.　　d. observation.

5. Which of the following is *not* a valid hypothesis?
   a. Children cry more when their mothers leave a room than when their fathers leave a room.
   b. College students like red jelly beans more than black jelly beans.
   c. More car accidents occur on rainy days than on sunny days.
   d. George Washington would have liked a Mac better than a PC.

2.2 Naturalistic Observation

Psychological research often takes place in carefully constructed experimental environments that do not allow for much variability in the way the research participants respond. For example, many kinds of research ask subjects to fill out questionnaires or to rate how likely they would be to respond in a particular way to a hypothetical situation. Some researchers worry that the limited response options that participants have in some experiments may not give psychologists much insight into the way people respond in more natural, everyday settings.

To overcome this problem, some psychologists conduct experiments that employ *naturalistic observation.* In these kinds of experiments, researchers try to create experimental environments that are similar to environments that might be encountered outside the laboratory. The researchers introduce the participants into the environments and then step back and observe how the participants respond.

Because the participants have more response options available in such situations, the experimenters must develop ways to categorize their responses. This process is usually referred to as *coding* the participants' behavior. This activity will give you an opportunity to code the behavior of infants in a classic experimental paradigm (the Strange Situation) using naturalistic observation.

TIPS

- It is very important that you pay careful attention as Dr. Martorell explains the different attachment styles and the kinds of behavior associated with each style. You will need this information for the observation portion of the activity.

- Once you begin the observation, remember that it is more important to observe the baby's behavior *after* the mother returns to the experimental room than whatever the baby is doing while the mother is out of the room.

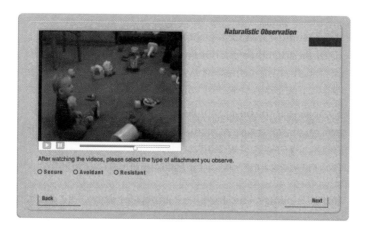

After watching the videos, please select the type of attachment you observe.

○ Secure   ○ Avoidant   ○ Resistant

Back   Next

REFLECTION QUESTION

You are interested in describing how children play during recess at school, with particular emphasis on both aggressive and cooperative play behaviors. Before you can be approved to run your observational research, the school principal wants to know how you plan to conduct the study. In your plan, you need to include where you will conduct the study and how you will record the behaviors. What are some common playground behaviors that you would record as "aggressive"? What behaviors would you record as "cooperative"?

MULTIPLE-CHOICE ITEMS

For decades, researchers have used the Strange Situation test to better understand attachment styles. In this situation, a primary caregiver leaves his or her child in a room with a stranger and several toys. After a few minutes, the primary caregiver returns. Researchers have noted several distinct patterns of behavior, both when the caregiver leaves and when the caregiver returns.

1. At first, Jake cries when his mother leaves the room but then plays contentedly with the toys. Upon his mother's return, Jake happily runs to her. Jake is demonstrating which style of attachment?
   a. secure
   b. avoidant
   c. resistant
   d. indifferent

2. Zoe does not notice when her mother leaves the room. When Zoe's mother returns, Zoe continues to play with the toys and does not respond to her mother's calls for her. Zoe is demonstrating which style of attachment?
   a. secure
   b. avoidant
   c. resistant
   d. indifferent

3. Claire is distressed when her mother leaves the room. When her mother returns, Claire goes to her but then pushes her away. Claire's mother can't seem to calm Claire down. Claire is demonstrating which style of attachment?
   a. secure
   b. avoidant
   c. resistant
   d. indifferent

4. One disadvantage to naturalistic observation is that
   a. the experimenter must wait for the appropriate conditions to occur.
   b. the experimental situation often does not appear like the "real world."
   c. participants tend to be dishonest when answering sensitive survey items.
   d. it takes place in a laboratory setting, which creates anxiety for participants.

5. Which of the following is the best example of a naturalistic observational study?
   a. Bill has participants learn a list of words and then tests their memory for the word list, either immediately or after a one-hour delay.
   b. Jill gives participants a survey to assess their shopping behavior over the course of one week.
   c. Audrey has participants record their most important daily event on a tape recorder for an entire semester every night before they go to sleep.
   d. Paige sits in the back of a classroom and systematically records the behavior of the students during a lecture.

2.3 Self-Report Bias in Surveys

Students of psychology are sometimes puzzled when they read that the causes of behavior are difficult to determine. A common response is, "If you want to know why Sarah cheated on her significant other, why not just ask her?" Although this kind of direct approach ought to be effective, psychologists have learned that the way people respond to surveys often reflects their biases rather than reality. The *self-report bias* is an example of this kind of bias. What you will see after you complete this activity—a simple survey on your attitude about important public issues—will probably surprise you. Your responses to the survey questions will make perfect sense to you. Presumably, the same would be true if your roommate took the survey. However, if we combined the survey results of many, many people, the sum of all of the responses would not provide an accurate picture of people's attitudes toward important world issues.

TIPS

- Think carefully about your own attitudes and the attitudes of others before responding to the survey questions. Consider the attitudes of many people you know and reports in the media when trying to assess the attitude of the general public.

- Ask several of your friends to complete the survey without revealing what the self-report bias is. Did their responses show evidence of a self-report bias?

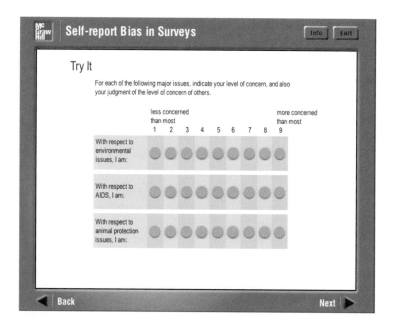

REFLECTION QUESTION

Review your personal results of the survey you just completed. Did you show the typical self-enhancement bias? Did you self-enhance in some domains more than in other domains? Why do you think this is? Why might self-enhancing be beneficial to a person? When might self-enhancing be detrimental?

MULTIPLE-CHOICE ITEMS

1. The self-enhancing bias suggests that
   a. we believe we are somewhat better than others in a variety of dimensions.
   b. when meeting new people, we exaggerate our positive characteristics.
   c. we attribute our successes to hard work; we attribute others' successes to luck.
   d. we tend to blame others for our failures.

2. Paul is completing a survey regarding academic issues. Based on what you know about self-enhancing biases, Paul is likely to
   a. claim he works harder than most students in his classes.
   b. claim he does not study as much as other students in his classes.
   c. claim that most students do better than he does in his classes.
   d. claim that few students do worse than he does in his classes.

3. People are likely to believe that
   a. they are more concerned about global warming than the general population.
   b. they are more concerned about homelessness than the general population.
   c. Both a and b
   d. Neither a nor b

4. If Betsy applied self-enhancement to listening skills, she would claim that
   a. she is better than most people at listening to others.
   b. she is about the same as others at listening to others.
   c. she is worse than most people at listening to others.
   d. she has no way of knowing how she compares to others.

2.4 Correlation

Correlation refers to the relationship between two variables, and also to a statistical procedure for determining the strength of the relationship between two variables. If two variables are highly correlated, then knowing how a person scores on one variable helps you predict how they will score on another variable. For example, there is a correlation between a child's temperament (anxious versus relaxed) and that of his or her parents. Knowing that a parent is very anxious helps you predict that the child is likely very anxious as well.

As this activity points out, it is important to remember that correlation does not imply causation. Just because two variables are highly correlated with one another does not mean that the presence of one causes the other to occur. Consider this hypothetical example: Let's assume that students who quickly finish their psychology midterm exams tend to do better than those who take longer. If these variables shared a causal relationship, it would imply that you should rush through your final exam as quickly as possible, because finishing your exam quickly would *cause* you to do better. Obviously, working faster will not ensure that you will do better. Instead, there is a third variable that explains the correlation: the amount of preparation. Students who are better prepared are likely to finish quickly and earn a higher grade. In this case, the amount of preparation is the variable that caused the observed correlation between the exam score and the time to complete the exam.

TIPS

- This activity gives you an opportunity to determine whether personal characteristics like happiness and friendliness are correlated with each other. Try to choose friends who differ from one another on the characteristics; in other words, do not choose people who all tend to be very happy or friendly. Choosing people who vary in these dimensions will make it more likely that strong correlations will emerge among the variables.

- As you complete this activity, try to guess which variables are most strongly correlated in your set of friends. At the end of the activity, the program will display the pairs of variables that show the strongest positive and negative correlations in your data set, so you can check to see if you are right.

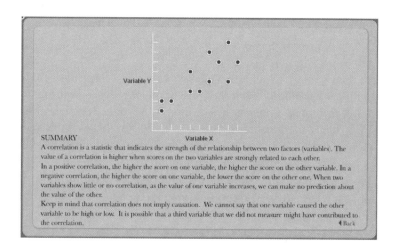

Variable Y

Variable X

SUMMARY

A correlation is a statistic that indicates the strength of the relationship between two factors (variables). The value of a correlation is higher when scores on the two variables are strongly related to each other. In a positive correlation, the higher the score on one variable, the higher the score on the other variable. In a negative correlation, the higher the score on one variable, the lower the score on the other one. When two variables show little or no correlation, as the value of one variable increases, we can make no prediction about the value of the other.

Keep in mind that correlation does not imply causation. We cannot say that one variable caused the other variable to be high or low. It is possible that a third variable that we did not measure might have contributed to the correlation.   ◀ Back

REFLECTION QUESTIONS

1. You have just been hired to create a pamphlet to help people understand what factors play a role in gaining and losing weight. There are several things that are positively correlated with a person's weight, several that are negatively correlated with a person's weight, and several that are not correlated with a person's weight. Provide an example of each of these correlations in your pamphlet.

2. Now consider the variable weight and the variable you selected that was positively correlated with weight. Generate a third variable that might be playing a role in the correlation. That is, what additional factor might be associated with both increasing weight *and* your selected variable? How would you discuss this issue in your pamphlet?

MULTIPLE-CHOICE ITEMS

1. Becca has been training for a marathon for several weeks. When she began her training, she could run a mile in twelve minutes. After two weeks of training, she could run a mile in ten minutes. After six weeks of training, she could run a mile in eight minutes. In this example, a(n) _____ exists between the number of weeks of training and the time to run a mile.
   a. positive correlation
   b. negative correlation
   c. neutral correlation
   d. absence of correlation

2. Candace has been feeling sad lately, so she has decided to volunteer at a soup kitchen in an attempt to lift her mood. Indeed, the more hours Candace spends at the soup kitchen, the happier she feels. Candace has noticed a(n) _____ correlation between her number of hours volunteering and her feelings of happiness.
   a. positive   b. negative   c. neutral   d. absence of

3. Matt believes that one good pair of shoes is all a person really needs. Matt has blond hair and one pair of shoes. Ellen believes that a person needs a good pair of running shoes, a pair of dress shoes, and a pair of slippers. Ellen has black hair and three pair of shoes. Imelda believes that the more shoes you own, the better! Imelda has brown hair

and seventy-nine pair of shoes. In this example, hair darkness and the number of shoes a person owns are _____ correlated.

a. positively   b. negatively   c. neutrally   d. not

4. Bill loves to chew gum when he studies for exams. He chewed two pieces of gum while studying for his first chemistry exam and received a C. Then he chewed four pieces of gum while studying for his second exam and received a B. He chewed nine pieces of gum while studying for his third exam and received an A. He now believes that chewing gum while studying definitely improves his test performance. According to correlational research, what is the problem with Bill's conclusion?

a. He is basing his conclusion solely on his chemistry-exam performance.

b. There appears to be no positive correlation in his example.

c. Correlation does not imply causation.

d. His method of study has no real-world validity.

5. Research has demonstrated a positive correlation between the number of hours of violent television watched and the amount of aggression in children. Based on these findings and what we know about correlational research, we can conclude that

a. watching violent television leads to aggression.

b. aggressive children mimic the violence they see on television shows.

c. parents who allow their children to view violent television shows are indirectly encouraging aggressive behavior.

d. None of the above

2.5 Designing an Experiment: Dependent and Independent Variables

Most psychologists use experiments to test their theories. The current activity is designed to give you a better sense of how psychology experiments are constructed. In particular, it will focus on the difference between *independent* variables and *dependent* variables in an experiment. In general, the independent variable is the factor that the experimenter controls; the dependent variable is the behavior that the experimenter is trying to measure. Let's look at an example. Most experiments start with a hypothesis that takes the following general form: "I think Factor X will influence Behavior Y." For example, one might hypothesize that the way a person is dressed (Factor X) will influence whether other people like her or him (Behavior Y). To test this hypothesis in an experiment, a researcher might introduce subjects to a confederate who is either dressed formally or informally. Then the subjects would be asked to rate how much they liked the confederate. In this example, the way the subject is dressed is the independent variable—the factor that the experimenter controls by manipulating the confederate's clothing. The subjects' ratings of how much they liked the confederate is the dependent variable. The experimenter has no direct control over the subjects' behavior, although it is hoped that the independent variable will indirectly affect their ratings. In this activity, you will have an opportunity to explore independent and dependent variables using a memory experiment.

- As each experiment is described, consider how you think the independent variable will influence the number of words that you remember. Do not focus solely on whether you think your memory will increase or decrease. You should also think about *why* you expect your performance to be better or worse. Psychological research is designed not only to understand how people behave but why they behave the way they do.

- Try to use the same basic strategy for memorizing the words across all the experimental conditions. Switching strategies will make it difficult to know if any change in the number of words that you remembered was a result of the different independent variable in each experiment or the different strategies that you used to memorize the words.

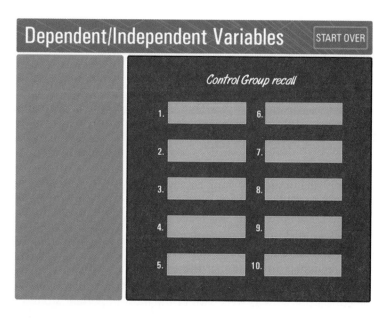

REFLECTION QUESTION

You have just been hired by the Crazy Cookie Factory to determine whether the new version of their choco-raisin-peanut-marshmallow cookies tastes better than the old version. Design an experiment that will provide the factory owners with an answer. Be sure to describe fully your hypothesis, the independent variable(s), and the dependent variable(s).

MULTIPLE-CHOICE ITEMS

1. The variable that a researcher manipulates in an experiment is called the
   _____ variable.
   a. dependent
   b. independent
   c. control
   d. spurious

2. Dr. Humor wonders if knock-knock jokes are funnier than "crossing the road" jokes. He has several people tell participants a series of both types of jokes and has the participants rate how funny they believe each joke to be. In this example, the dependent variable is
   a. the type of joke.
   b. the order of the presentation of the jokes.
   c. the participants' humor ratings.
   d. the person telling the jokes.

3. After reading that taking an afternoon nap improves mood, Hilda wonders whether sleeping in on the weekend would have the same effect. Hilda has generated a(n)
   a. dependent variable.
   b. independent variable.
   c. hypothesis.
   d. validation.

4. Researchers have found that using flash cards is a better study method than highlighting key terms in a textbook. In this example, the independent variable is
   a. test scores.
   b. the study method.
   c. Both a and b
   d. Neither a nor b

2.6 Ethical Dilemmas

From 1932 until 1972, hundreds of poor, largely illiterate African American men were denied treatment for syphilis, a painful and frequently fatal disease. The decision to deny treatment to these individuals was made in the name of science. The physicians running the study wanted to learn more about how the disease progressed. Although one could claim that learning more about how syphilis attacks the body was a valuable goal, it is impossible to argue that the ends of this research program justified the means. It is important to note that psychological research has been plagued by questionable ethical practices as well. Two of the most important studies in the history of social psychology—Milgram's obedience study and Zimbardo's Stanford prison study—have been strongly criticized for the way the subjects were treated (see Activities 15.5 and 15.6).

In response to these and other ethical abuses made by medical and psychological researchers, the federal government imposed standards for the ethical treatment of human subjects. Every psychological experiment that is conducted must now be approved by an institutional review board (IRB). Every college or university that conducts research has an IRB whose job is to ensure that every research project conforms to certain standards of ethical treatment. The activity that you are about to complete describes these standards and gives you an opportunity to apply them to evaluate some proposed research projects.

- The activity does not mention one important criterion that IRBs use to judge research proposals: minimal risk. *Minimal risk* means that participating in the study poses no harm greater than what a person might encounter in their everyday life.

- An IRB might relax some requirements if a study poses no more than minimal risk to the subjects. Be aware of this as you read and evaluate whether the research scenarios in this activity violate any ethical principles.

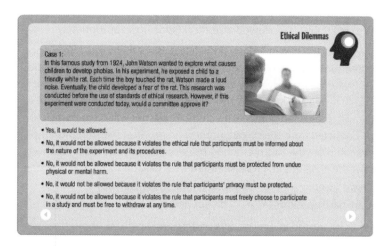

REFLECTION QUESTIONS

1. Deception in psychological experiments has always been a controversial issue because it is sometimes necessary for the validity of an experiment and can sometimes be harmful. Generate an example where deception makes sense in light of the experimental procedure. Generate an example where deception is misused and causes more harm than good.

2. Go online to http://www.cdc.gov/tuskegee/timeline.htm and read more about the Tuskegee syphilis study. How did the researchers fail? How might one ethically conduct this kind of research?

MULTIPLE-CHOICE ITEMS

1. All of the following are APA ethical standards for psychology experiments *except:*
    a. Participants must be informed of the nature of the experiment and its procedures.
    b. Participants must be able to withdraw from the experiment at any time without penalty.
    c. Participants must be allowed to select the conditions of the experiment in which they participate.
    d. Participants must be protected from physical or mental harm.

2. John is planning on conducting an experiment to see how men and women differ in geography performance. After describing the study to the participants, he gives them a written geography test. To make sure he doesn't mix up his data, he has each person write his or her name at the top of the test. Before John leaves the room, he instructs the participants to drop their exams in an open box outside his office door so that he can pick them up when he returns later that week. John's study should

   a. not be approved because he has violated the ethical standard of protection from harm.

   b. not be approved because he has violated the ethical standard of confidentiality/privacy.

   c. not be approved because he has incorporated unnecessary deception in his study.

   d. be approved. John has followed all ethical guidelines appropriately.

3. Professor Memory is examining how time delays affect memory performance. He decides to use students in his psychology course as his subjects. During a class session, he tells the students about the study. They will take two memory tests with an hour interval between each test. As an incentive, he informs the class that those who are willing to participate will receive ten points extra credit. Those not willing to participate will have ten points deducted from their overall course grade. After the students who choose to participate complete the two memory tests anonymously, Professor Memory explains the basis for the experiment. Professor Memory is violating which ethical standard?

   a. informed consent

   b. voluntary participation

   c. confidentiality/privacy

   d. debriefing

4. Dr. Sanders is interested in how people understand feedback about their performance and incorporate it into their view of themselves. She has large groups of participants take a bogus personality test and then, in front of the group, tells them individually whether their scores were very high, average, or very low. She also tells them that their scores on the test accurately predict future life success. Dr. Sanders then has the participants write a short paragraph describing their personal strengths and weaknesses. At the end of the study, the participants turn in their paragraphs and are excused. At no time does Dr. Sanders inform them that the test and feedback were actually false. In fact, she never tells them about the nature of the study. Dr. Sanders's study violates which ethical standards?

   a. protection from harm

   b. informed consent

   c. confidentiality/privacy

   d. debriefing

   e. All of the above

5. Deception in psychological research

   a. should never be allowed.

   b. should always be allowed.

   c. should be allowed only if participants are never informed of the nature of the study at its conclusion.

   d. should be allowed only if the procedure yields a significant social benefit and causes, at the most, only minimal harm.

CHAPTER THREE

The Brain and Behavior

3.1 The Structure of Neurons

The nervous system is a vast, complex communication network. In many ways, our nervous system is like the man-made communication systems we're all familiar with. How does cable television reach your home? Electrical signals are sent across a network of wires. Your television interprets those electrical signals, enabling you to see your favorite programs.

Our nervous system works in a similar manner. Electrical signals (nerve impulses, or action potentials) are sent across a network of wires (neurons). These impulses are interpreted by the brain and by our arms, legs, and vital organs. The animation in this activity provides an example. The needle prick starts a neural signal that is transmitted via neurons to the brain. The brain interprets this signal as pain and sends a neural signal as a response to the hand; the muscles in the hand interpret the neural signal as an instruction to move the hand away from the needle.

The rest of this activity presents some of the details of how signals are transmitted within and between neurons. There are two important things to notice. First, there is no such thing as a "strong" or a "weak" action potential. We refer to this aspect of neural activity as the *all-or-none law*. A stimulus is either strong enough to elicit an action potential (*all*) or it is too weak to produce any neural response (*none*). Second, neurons do not communicate with one another directly. There are gaps, called *synapses*, between neurons. The electrical signal within the neuron is transmitted across these gaps by chemicals that are released into the synapse. These chemicals are called *neurotransmitters*.

TIPS

- Be sure to understand the all-or-none law. Figure out the fewest times you must stimulate the virtual neuron to elicit an action potential. Stimulating the neuron fewer times does not generate a weaker action potential; it produces no response whatsoever. Similarly, stimulating the neuron additional times does not produce a stronger action potential; the "size" of the neural response is exactly the same.

- Neurotransmitters do not all have the same effect when released into the synapse. Some increase the likelihood that an action potential will be generated by the next neuron; some decrease the likelihood that an action potential will be generated by the next neuron. This allows the nervous system to fine-tune our responses to the environment.

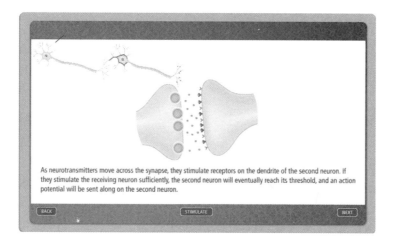

As neurotransmitters move across the synapse, they stimulate receptors on the dendrite of the second neuron. If they stimulate the receiving neuron sufficiently, the second neuron will eventually reach its threshold, and an action potential will be sent along on the second neuron.

BACK   STIMULATE   NEXT

REFLECTION QUESTIONS

1. Billy is playing outside, and a mosquito lands on his arm. He quickly slaps it away with his other hand. How are neural signals, neurons, and the brain involved in this process? What three basic steps must occur?

2. Neural communication occurs in two ways: communication within a neuron and communication between two neurons. What is the process of communication within a neuron (from the moment the dendrite receives a signal)? What is the process of communication between two neurons?

MULTIPLE-CHOICE ITEMS

1. The protective fatty coating(s) that encase(s) the axon and increase(s) the speed of the electrical signal as it travels within a neuron is (are) the
   a. myelin sheath.   c. cell body.
   b. terminal buttons.   d. synapse.

2. Which of the following is true about the action potential?
   a. Its speed is determined by the number of terminal buttons receiving the signal.
   b. It is an all-or-nothing response determined by the strength of the signal.
   c. It can be slowed down when specific neurotransmitters are released.
   d. It becomes larger as the signal strength becomes stronger.

3. The _____ send(s) messages to other neurons.
   a. dendrites   c. myelin sheath
   b. terminal buttons   d. cell body

4. _____ are the fibers that receive signals from other neurons.
   a. Terminal buttons   c. Axons
   b. Neurotransmitters   d. Dendrites

5. Dendrites receive stimulus input from
   - a. other neurons.
   - b. the outside world.
   - c. Both a and b
   - d. Neither a nor b

6. When the action potential reaches the end of the axon, neurotransmitters are released directly into the _____
   - a. dendrites of the receiving neuron.
   - b. synapse between two neurons.
   - c. cell body of the receiving neuron.
   - d. axons of the receiving neuron.

3.2 Areas and Functions of the Brain

One of the most elementary questions in the field of psychology is how the brain is organized. Neuroscientists have discovered that certain areas of the brain tend to be associated with certain kinds of behaviors. This activity gives you an opportunity to learn about the functions of some of the major areas of the brain. It is important to remember that although particular functions may be ascribed to specific areas in the brain, any reasonably complex behavior is going to require multiple brain areas working together. For example, telling a friend what you did last night involves brain areas related to memory, language, narrative construction, imagery, and so forth. Thus, knowing what areas of the brain are associated with what behaviors is only a first step in understanding how the brain controls behavior. Neuroscientists are currently trying to understand how these various areas are coordinated and to identify the "neural code" that the brain uses to represent and transmit information.

TIPS

- To prepare for the activity quiz, make sure you review the names, locations, and functions of each brain area. The quiz will ask you to locate areas based on name and function, so you will need to know all three features of each brain area.

- One interesting aspect of brain organization is how the brain evolved. In general, the brain has evolved from the brain stem (medulla) upward and outward. Areas close to the brain stem tend to be associated with basic survival (sleep, wakefulness, breathing), whereas areas farther from the brain stem tend to be associated with more complex, "human" behaviors like language and logical reasoning.

- The corpus callosum connects the left and right hemispheres of the brain. Although the two halves of the brain are anatomically symmetrical, the left and right hemispheres do not always serve exactly the same functions. For example, language is governed by the left hemisphere in the majority of right-handed people. For more information on differences between the two hemispheres, see Activity 3.3, "Brain Lateralization."

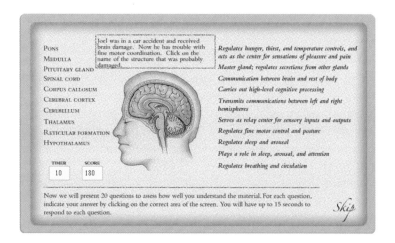

REFLECTION QUESTIONS

1. You are a neurologist who trains medical students working with head-injury patients. You want them to be able to understand how different symptomatology relates to injuries to different parts of the brain. Create three patient complaints and the parts of the brain that have most likely been injured, based on the complaints.

2. What would you caution your students regarding the precise relationships between a simple behavior and the parts of the brain that regulate it?

MULTIPLE-CHOICE ITEMS

1. To relieve epileptic seizures, Bill has had his corpus callosum severed. Now Bill has difficulty
   a. regulating fine-motor control.
   b. sleeping and waking appropriately.
   c. communicating between his right and left hemispheres.
   d. breathing.

2. Leroy is a football player who suffered a head injury during a practice. He now has difficulty sewing a button onto a shirt. Leroy most likely had damage to his
   a. cerebellum.   c. medulla.
   b. hypothalamus.   d. reticular formation.

3. Ella is always hungry, no matter how much she eats. Which part of her brain might be functioning improperly?
   a. pons
   b. cerebellum
   c. thalamus
   d. hypothalamus

4. Deciding which chapters to review for an upcoming exam is regulated by the
   a. hypothalamus.
   b. pituitary gland.
   c. cerebral cortex.
   d. pons.

5. John lifts a box and places it on a shelf. Based on our current understanding of brain functioning,
   a. neuroscientists can pinpoint the exact part of the brain responsible for this activity.
   b. neuroscientists have no way of determining the areas of the brain involved in this activity.
   c. neuroscientists know that a single part of the brain is responsible for this activity; they just have not localized it yet.
   d. neuroscientists recognize that even simple behaviors such as lifting a box require the action of many parts of the brain.

3.3 Brain Lateralization

The human brain is symmetrical. It consists of two halves: the left and the right hemispheres. Although the structures in the two sides of the brain are identical, they do not always perform exactly the same functions. Normally, we are unaware of the way mental work is shared by the two hemispheres because our actions are coordinated very well by the corpus callosum, a bundle of nerve fibers that quickly transmits information from one hemisphere to the other.

However, there are experimental situations that allow us to glimpse our two hemispheres working together or apart. This activity is one example. Before you begin, it is important to know that most behaviors involving the left side of our body are handled by the right hemisphere, and vice versa. Thus, when you are pressing the space bar in the activity with your *right* hand, the motor areas in the *left* hemisphere are active. When you press the space bar with your *left* hand, the motor areas in the *right* hemisphere are active.

TIPS

- As you watch the video, notice that for some behaviors (e.g., language) PET-scan activity is observed in only one hemisphere. For other behaviors, like vision and hearing, activity is recorded in both hemispheres simultaneously.

- When completing the experiment, be sure to hit the space bar with one finger on each hand. Use the same finger (on either the left or the right hand) for all four trials. This is important to make sure that differences from trial to trial are not due to your switching the way in which you press the space bar.

- Remember that language tends to be more localized in people who are strongly right-handed. If you are left-handed or mixed-handed (you do some things better with your left hand and some better with your right), language is less likely to be strongly localized in the left hemisphere, so you will be less likely to see the expected effect.

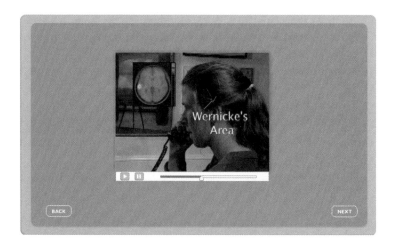

REFLECTION QUESTION

Research has shown that when someone is driving and talking on a cell phone, they are most likely holding the cell phone with the right hand and holding the steering wheel (i.e., driving) with the left hand. Based on what you learned in the interactive exercise, why is this a bad practice?

MULTIPLE-CHOICE ITEMS

1. Joan is having a conversation with her friend Maria. When Joan is speaking to Maria, _____ area of the brain becomes active. When Joan is listening to Maria, _____ area of the brain becomes active.
   a. Wernicke's; Broca's
   b. Broca's; Wernicke's
   c. Wernicke's; Wernicke's
   d. Broca's; Broca's

2. Baby Lulu loves touching her silk blanket. She sees it next to her and reaches for it, thereby stimulating her _____ cortex. When she feels the silky threads of the blanket, her _____ cortex is stimulated.
   a. sensory; sensory
   b. sensory; motor
   c. motor; sensory
   d. motor; motor

3. According to the exercise on interference in brain activity, a person will have the most interference when
   a. reading a magazine while eating potato chips with the left hand.
   b. reading a magazine while eating potato chips with the right hand.
   c. listening to a story while eating potato chips with the right hand.
   d. All of the above are equally interfering.

4. Following a serious car accident, in which Joe suffered a head injury, he is no longer able to understand the information he reads aloud. Joe has most likely suffered trauma to which part of the brain?

   a. Wernicke's area   c. motor cortex

   b. visual cortex   d. Broca's area

5. Saleem reads a sentence aloud from a book. Based on what we know about brain function,

   a. neuroscientists can pinpoint the exact location of the brain that is responsible for this simple activity.

   b. even simple behaviors such as this are based on interconnections among sets of neurons located in many areas of the brain.

   c. neuroscientists do not have the technology to "see" the activity of the brain, so it is impossible to know which areas of the brain are responsible for various behaviors.

   d. None of the above

3.4 Localization of Function: Second-Language Learning and Brain Plasticity

Sherlock Holmes likened his memory to an attic. When a new piece of information is encountered, it is stored in the brain much like boxes of old books and clothes. However, modern psychologists reject Holmes's analogy, for several reasons. One of the most important ways the attic analogy fails is that boxes in an attic remain relatively fixed and unchanged even as new boxes enter the attic. In contrast, the organization of our brain is constantly changing as new experiences modify connections between neurons. The constant reorganization that occurs as we encounter new experiences is called *plasticity*. The current activity will demonstrate how experience influences the way the brain processes language. As you will see, the age at which you learn a language (think about first versus second languages) influences where in the brain vocabulary and grammatical rules are represented.

TIPS

- Before beginning this activity, try to predict which areas of the brain are going to be involved in retaining vocabulary and grammar. Do you think the cortical areas or more primitive brain structures are going to be involved? This activity will give you an opportunity to check your prediction.

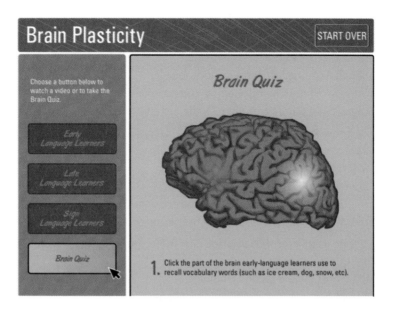

REFLECTION QUESTION

Some theorists believe that the way a second language is acquired may account for differences in linguistic representation. Whereas early language acquisition tends to be informal (picked up by living in a place that uses a new language), late language acquisition tends to be formal (learned in a classroom environment). How might you conduct an experiment to determine whether formal training influences the way second languages are represented in the brain? What would you predict for the results of your experiment?

MULTIPLE-CHOICE ITEMS

1. The difference between "early" and "late" language learning is that the "early" period is considered to occur prior to
   a. 1 year of age.
   b. 7 years of age.
   c. the beginning of puberty.
   d. the end of puberty.

2. For people who learn a second language early in life, the brain areas involved in grammar
   a. overlap for the first and second language.
   b. are different for the first and second language.
   c. are located in different hemispheres in the occipital lobe.
   d. are located in the same hemisphere in the occipital lobe.

3. For people who learn a second language later in life, the brain areas involved in grammar
   a. overlap for the first and second language.
   b. are different from the first and second language.
   c. are located in different hemispheres in the occipital lobe.
   d. are located in the same hemisphere in the occipital lobe.

4. For people who learn a second language early in life, the brain areas involved in vocabulary
   a. overlap for the first and second language.
   b. are different from the first and second language.
   c. are located in different hemispheres in the occipital lobe.
   d. are located in the same hemisphere in the occipital lobe.

5. For people who learn a second language later in life, the brain areas involved in vocabulary
   a. overlap for the first and second language.
   b. are different from the first and second language.
   c. are located in different hemispheres in the occipital lobe.
   d. are located in the same hemisphere in the occipital lobe.

CHAPTER FOUR

Sensation and Perception

4.1 Weber's Law

Let's say I gave you the opportunity to earn $10 by completing a five-minute question-naire or $110 by completing a sixty-minute questionnaire. Which would you choose? What if you were choosing between earning $1,000 for completing a five-minute ques-tionnaire versus $1,100 for completing a sixty-minute questionnaire? In both cases the difference between the earnings for the long and short questionnaire is $100, but if you are like most people, you would be more likely to choose the long questionnaire in the first case than in the second case.

There are various ways to understand why people might be more likely to choose the long questionnaire in the first set of choices, but one explanation is that the additional $100 seems more valuable in comparison to $10 than it does in comparison to $1,000. This explanation is analogous to Weber's law, which describes how people perceive dif-ferences between similar stimuli. As you will see in this activity, a constant difference in loudness seems greater when two quiet stimuli are compared than when two loud stimuli are compared. The same relationship holds true for our other senses, includ-ing vision, taste, temperature, and weight. Because Weber's law is applicable across so many of our senses, psychologists generally believe that our perceptual system evolved to help us detect changes in the magnitude of environmental stimuli.

TIPS

- Try to avoid using "Cannot tell a difference" as a response option. You are more likely to see the expected pattern if you force yourself to choose one stimulus or another.

- Compare your results against chance performance. Chance performance represents the probability of choosing the correct response if you were guessing without listen-ing to the stimuli. If you used all three response options, chance responding would be 33 percent (1 out of 3). If you eliminated the "Cannot tell a difference" option, chance responding would be 50 percent (1 out of 2). Were you better than chance for the loud stimuli? Were you better than chance for the soft stimuli? If you scored at or below chance, it means that you could not distinguish the difference between the two sounds any better than someone who had not listened to the stimuli but was forced to guess at random.

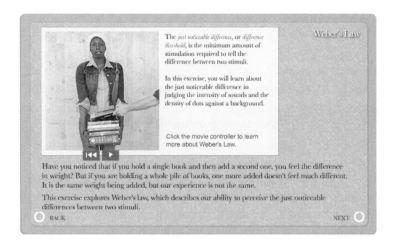

The *just noticeable difference*, or *difference threshold*, is the minimum amount of stimulation required to tell the difference between two stimuli.

In this exercise, you will learn about the just noticeable difference in judging the intensity of sounds and the density of dots against a background.

Click the movie controller to learn more about Weber's Law.

Weber's Law

Have you noticed that if you hold a single book and then add a second one, you feel the difference in weight? But if you are holding a whole pile of books, one more added doesn't feel much different. It is the same weight being added, but our experience is not the same.

This exercise explores Weber's law, which describes our ability to perceive the just noticeable differences between two stimuli.

BACK   NEXT

REFLECTION QUESTION

Miss Lulu, the head preschool teacher at the Super-Duper School, is having a problem with little Eric. Eric loves to talk all the time. He talks at play time, at sharing time, at rest time, and at music time. Miss Lulu is only really bothered by Eric's talking during rest time, even though Eric does not talk any louder during rest time than he does at other times of the day. According to Weber's law, why does Eric's talking bother Miss Lulu the most during rest time? What time of day do you think Miss Lulu would be least bothered by Eric's talking?

MULTIPLE-CHOICE ITEMS

1. The minimum amount of stimulation required to tell the difference between two stimuli is called the
   a. difference threshold.   c. perceptual threshold.
   b. absolute threshold.   d. minimal stimulation threshold.

2. According to Weber's law, you are more likely to detect a difference in sound between
   a. 2 and 4 decibels.   c. 4 and 6 decibels.
   b. 4 and 5 decibels.   d. 4 and 7 decibels.

3. Julia is holding a basket of apples that weighs 5 pounds. Sammy keeps adding more apples to Julia's basket and asks her to tell him when she notices that the basket is heavier. Julia notices a difference when the basket's weight reaches 6 pounds. Now Julia is holding a basket of apples weighing 10 pounds. According to Weber's law, how much additional weight in apples must be added for Julia to notice a difference?
   a. 1 pound
   b. 1.5 pounds
   c. 2 pounds
   d. It is impossible to calculate.

4. Based on what you have learned about Weber's law and just noticeable differences,
   a. the magnitude of the stimulus does not affect the ability to detect changes in stimulus intensity.
   b. it is easier to detect changes in stimulus intensity when the intensities are high.
   c. it is easier to detect changes in stimulus intensity when the intensities are low.
   d. it depends on the sensory domain as to whether it is easier to detect changes in stimulus intensities for low intensities versus high intensities.

5. Tammy wants to attend a concert of her favorite duo, Queen Tunius and the Jake-man. Unfortunately, she does not have a ticket. She has decided to sneak into the concert but is worried she might get caught because a security guard is sitting in the concert hall watching for trespassers. According to Weber's law,
   a. Tammy should sneak into the concert hall before any of the rest of the audience arrives.
   b. Tammy should sneak into the concert hall after about 10 of the 500 audience members arrive.
   c. Tammy should wait until most of the audience is in the concert hall before she sneaks in.
   d. Weber's law is not helpful in making a decision in this example.

4.2 How Do We See?

The eye is a complex sensory organ that transforms light from the outside world into our sense of vision. Light passes through many structures on its journey through the eye. This activity was designed to teach you the various structures in the eye and how they contribute to vision. The complexity of the process is nicely illustrated by the different cells in the retina, the layer of cells in the back of the eye that captures the light that is funneled through the pupil. The retina consists of two kinds of cells, rods and cones, that are sensitive to different aspects of the visual world. Whereas cones are primarily responsible for color vision, rods are specialized for detecting motion.

Of course, the responses of the various structures of the eye are just the first step in creating our sense of vision. The neural signals that originate in the optic nerve are then passed through several areas of the brain, including the thalamus, to their ultimate destination: the occipital cortex (located at the back of the brain). The occipital cortex is where much of the higher-level analysis of the visual signal is done. In other words, the occipital cortex is where neural signals are turned into our visual understanding of the world.

TIPS

- Study the diagram of the eye carefully. Then use the video to test how much you have learned. As Dr. Murthy shows the three-dimensional model of the eye, try to identify the various structures of the eye before he shows their locations and describes their functions.
- You might be surprised to learn that our retinas have a blind spot where the optic nerve begins. Why don't we see a small black spot as we look around the world? It's because our eyes are constantly moving. The brain uses this motion to fill in the missing information, so what we see is one clear, uninterrupted view of the world.

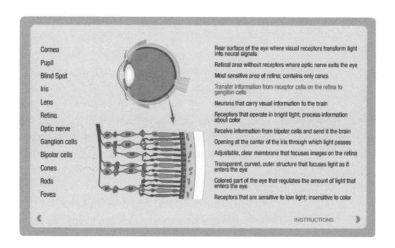

Cornea	Rear surface of the eye where visual receptors transform light into neural signals
Pupil	Retinal area without receptors where optic nerve exits the eye
Blind Spot	Most sensitive area of retina; contains only cones
Iris	Transfer information from receptor cells on the retina to ganglion cells
Lens	Neurons that carry visual information to the brain
Retina	Receptors that operate in bright light; process information about color
Optic nerve	Receive information from bipolar cells and send it the brain
Ganglion cells	Opening at the center of the iris through which light passes
Bipolar cells	Adjustable, clear membrane that focuses images on the retina
Cones	Transparent, curved, outer structure that focuses light as it enters the eye
Rods	Colored part of the eye that regulates the amount of light that enters the eye
Fovea	Receptors that are sensitive to low light; insensitive to color

INSTRUCTIONS

REFLECTION QUESTION

When we "see" an object, it is the result many structures in the eye working in a step-by-step process. Trace this process from light first entering the eye to that visual information being relayed to the brain. Be sure to include the following structures in your description: retina, cornea, ganglion cells, photoreceptors, lens, iris, bipolar cells, and optic nerve.

MULTIPLE-CHOICE ITEMS

1. Sammy is color-blind. Which of his photoreceptors are not functioning properly?
   a. rods
   b. cones
   c. bipolar cells
   d. ganglion cells

2. As you leave a movie theater and enter a well-lit lobby, your pupils become smaller to adjust to the increase in light. What structure of the eye controls this process?
   a. cornea
   b. lens
   c. iris
   d. retina

3. Visual information is relayed to the brain via the
   a. ganglion cells.
   b. bipolar cells.
   c. fovea.
   d. optic nerve.

4. _____ are highly sensitive to color; _____ are insensitive to color.
   a. Rods; cones
   b. Cones; rods
   c. Ganglion cells; bipolar cells
   d. Bipolar cells, ganglion cells

5. The blind spot refers to
   a. the minimal size the pupil can retract to in the brightest light conditions.
   b. the area of the retina where no cones are present.
   c. an inability to see objects outside of one's peripheral view.
   d. the part of the retina where the optic nerve exits the eye and no receptors exist.

4.3 Basic Sensory Processes

One of the most important jobs that our brain does for us is to help us make sense of the world. This ability allows us to locate necessary resources like food, water, and friends; it also helps us avoid dangers in the world like predators, enemies, and steep cliffs. The four sensory-processing videos collected here provide some insights into how these different sensory systems evolved. There are obvious differences, but some of the similarities are worth noting. In all cases, the job of the sensory system is to take a physical stimulus from the outside world and translate it into an electrochemical signal in the brain. This signal is interpreted as color or pressure or chocolate pudding.

An important but often difficult-to-understand point is that we do not experience our physical environment directly. All of our experiences are mediated by brain activity. What we experience are responses based on how our brains interpret the physical stimuli that we encounter. Popular music provides an example that helps clarify this point. The physical stimulus of a particular song is the same when it reaches your ears as when it reaches your parents' ears. However, your brain may interpret this stimulus very differently from how it is interpreted by your parents' brains. Thus, whereas you may love the latest hit from the Foo Fighters when you hear it on the radio, your parents may loudly tell you to "turn that noise down."

TIPS

- The details of how any one of these systems work are extremely complicated, and we still have a great deal to learn about the specifics of each system. Still, it is important to understand how a physical stimulus is translated into an electrochemical signal. Pay particular attention to this transition for each sensory system.

- The video on tactile information processing talks about how tactile information is represented for different parts of the body. Think about how different sensory systems might be represented for other animals; for example, nocturnal animals, which rely on smell more than vision, or birds of prey, which rely heavily on vision to locate prey.

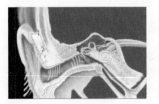 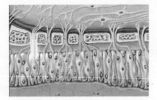 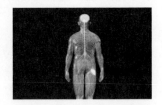

REFLECTION QUESTION

One important—and sometimes difficult to grasp—aspect of sensory processing is that we do not directly experience our physical environment. Our brains mediate our experience of the world. There is no red light in the world. We perceive certain wavelengths of light as red because of the way our visual system is designed. If we were to retune the system, red light might appear greenish, as is the case for some people who are color-blind. Given that our brains interpret the physical world for us and that everyone's brain is unique, can we be sure that everyone perceives the world the same way? Even though you and I both claim that a stop sign is red, can we be sure that we both perceive the redness of the sign in the same way?

MULTIPLE-CHOICE ITEMS

1. Relative to our other senses, the largest portion of our cortex is devoted to
   a. audition.
   b. olfaction.
   c. touch.
   d. vision.

2. The _____ system has direct neural connections to emotional and memory areas of the brain.
   a. auditory
   b. olfactory
   c. tactile
   d. visual

3. Cortical regions devoted to the sense of touch form a mental map of our bodies. Which of the following statements about this mental map is true?
   a. The amount of area in the cortex devoted to a particular body part is proportional to the size of that body part. Large body parts take up lots of space in the cortex; small body parts, relatively little space.
   b. The area of cortex devoted to a particular body part is determined by how sensitive that body part is. For example, a great deal of cortex is devoted to the fingers and the face.
   c. The size and arrangement of the cortex shows little variability across people.
   d. Experience has little effect on the way body parts are represented in the cortex.

4. Our sense of hearing requires that we transform
   a. an electrical signal into a chemical signal.
   b. a chemical signal into an electrical signal.
   c. a mechanical signal into an electrical signal.
   d. an electrical signal into a mechanical signal.

5. Which of the following statements best reflects the way rods and cones contribute to our sense of vision?
   a. Rods and cones generally perform the same function, but cones are more sensitive than rods.
   b. Rods are specialized for color vision; cones, for detecting light and dark.
   c. Cones are specialized for color vision; rods, for detecting light and dark.
   d. None of the above

4.4 Perception: Integrating the Senses

During our daily routines, we effortlessly integrate sensory information into a single unified representation of the world. For example, we perceive the noise made by a fan and know that the same object is producing the cool breeze that we feel. One question that psychologists have been pursuing is where in the brain this integration takes place. What part of the brain is responsible for taking inputs from the auditory, visual, olfactory, and tactile cortexes and combining them to form our unified perception of the outside world? One current line of reasoning holds that this mysterious "sensory integration" portion of the brain simply does not exist. In this video, Dr. Antonio Demasio will explain how we make sense of the world, given that no single part of the brain organizes all of our perceptions for us. The video will also discuss how our perception of the world is altered by experience, particularly the effects of culture.

TIPS

- One point that Dr. Demasio makes that may be confusing is the difference between the perception of an object and a later memory of that object. In other words, the brain activity that ccurs when you see Dr. Demasio's video is similar to, but not the same as, the brain activity that will occur an hour or so from now if you try to remember then what Dr. Demasio looked like or what his voice sounded like.

- The video describes how culture influences our perception, particularly the kinds of foods that we are willing to eat. But it may not be clear from the video that these norms can change with experience. For example, being served raw fish would have elicited groans from most people in the United States twenty to thirty years ago, but sushi is now a very popular cuisine. This suggests that the perceptual systems in American people are not wired differently from those in Japanese people. Rather, experiences influence the way links in the system are formed.

 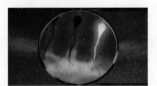 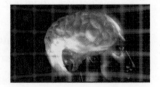

REFLECTION QUESTION

It is often said that traveling to new places and new countries "broadens one's horizons." What mechanisms might a cognitive psychologist propose to explain how travel broadens one's perceptions?

MULTIPLE-CHOICE ITEMS

1. According to Dr. Demasio, sensory integration
   a. occurs in the thalamus.
   b. occurs in the hypothalamus.
   c. occurs in the hippocampus.
   d. does not take place in any single brain region.

2. When Sally entered her first-year college dorm, she was very nervous about meeting her new roommate, Alex. Fortunately, Sally and Alex liked each other immediately. Later that night, Sally's Mom asked her to describe her roommate. In order to remember her roommate, Sally's brain
   a. accessed a memory of Alex that was stored at the time of their meeting.
   b. generated separate mental images of Alex's appearance, voice, and so forth and then fused these images together into a single memory.
   c. tried to re-create the pattern of neural activity that had first allowed Sally to perceive Alex when they met.
   d. sent a neural signal to Sally's mouth instructing her to say, "Well, like you know, she's like pretty cool."

3. Experiencing the world aids perception by
   a. enabling us to use what we know about the world to interpret new stimuli.
   b. enabling us to compare our perceptions with those of others around us.
   c. enabling us to treat every incoming stimulus as new and unique.
   d. enabling us to store new information without regard to old information.

4. People from the same culture are likely to perceive a stimulus in the same way because people from the same culture
   a. share similar genes.
   b. share similar experiences.
   c. are not sensitive to environmental influences.
   d. are not sensitive to biological influences.

5. The fact that people from Western cultures typically do not eat insects or snakes indicates that people from Western cultures
   a. are more civilized than other people.
   b. are less adventurous than other people.
   c. have not traveled extensively enough.
   d. have had different experiences than other people.

4.5 Top-Down versus Bottom-Up Processing

What happens when people we know well change their appearance dramatically by cutting their hair short, getting contact lenses, or shaving their beard or moustache? Sometimes these changes are so striking that we may walk right past these people without recognizing them. At other times we recognize that something about their appearance has changed, but we have great difficulty identifying exactly what is new. These two scenarios can both occur because we use more than one kind of information to recognize objects in our environment: *top-down processing* and *bottom-up processing*. Briefly, bottom-up processing refers to the use of physical features to identify stimuli. Top-down processing involves using general world knowledge and expectations to identify stimuli. This activity will give you an opportunity to see how both types of processing work simultaneously to allow you to make sense of the world around you.

TIPS

- Be sure to use the quote to help you guess the phrase.
- After you complete this activity, return to the scenarios presented in the paragraph above. Does failing to recognize that someone has shaved his beard demonstrate top-down or bottom-up processing? What about failing to recognize a person because of a new haircut?

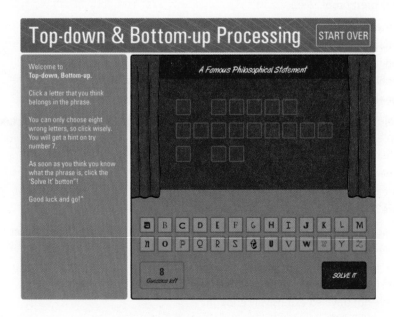

REFLECTION QUESTION

There are no known cases of people losing the ability to engage in either top-down or bottom-up processing, but imagine that you were faced with the prospect of losing one or the other. Which mode of processing would be more difficult to live without? Why?

MULTIPLE-CHOICE ITEMS

1. Your best friend, Marc, leaves you a voice mail, asking if he can change the restaurant where you had agreed to meet him for dinner. Just as he mentions the new place where he wants to eat, his voice is obscured by a loud conversation going on in the background. It sounded like Marc said Antonio's, a restaurant that you eat at frequently with Marc. So you go to Antonio's, and sure enough, Marc is there waiting for you. This situation illustrates
   a. top-down processing.   c. side-to-side processing.
   b. bottom-up processing.   d. over-the-hill processing.

2. Just for fun, you play Marc's message for your mother, who does not know Marc or the restaurants that you frequent. She should be
   a. less likely to identify the name of the restaurant because she cannot employ top-down processing.
   b. more likely to identify the name of the restaurant because she cannot employ top-down processing.
   c. less likely to identify the name of the restaurant because she cannot employ bottom-up processing.
   d. more likely to identify the name of the restaurant because she cannot employ bottom-up processing.

3. In this activity, the quotes helped by enabling you to use
   a. top-down processing.   c. over-the-top processing.
   b. bottom-up processing.   d. in-through-the-out-door processing.

4. You went to the Army–Navy football game to meet your friend Kurt, who attends the Naval Academy. Finding Kurt turns out to be a problem because half of the people at the game are approximately six feet tall with similar haircuts and wearing Naval Academy uniforms (including hats, which are called "covers" at the Naval Academy). The difficulty you have in finding Kurt occurs because you cannot use
   a. top-down processing.   c. ear-to-ear processing.
   b. bottom-up processing.   d. head-to-toe processing.

5. A person who has lost his or her sense of vision can still recognize people by their voices. Such a person uses
   a. top-down processes to recognize people.
   b. bottom-up processes to recognize people.
   c. neither top-down nor bottom-up processes to recognize people.
   d. both top-down and bottom-up processes to recognize people.

4.6 Depth Perception

One of the most common misconceptions about how people perceive the world is that our senses simply reconstruct the physical world for us. The reasons for this misconception are quite simple. In most everyday settings, our senses do give us accurate information about the environment. If we smell popcorn, there is a very good chance that our roommate or next-door neighbor has just pulled a bag of popcorn out of the microwave. If we see smoke, there usually is a fire. We are able to navigate through our world effortlessly without bumping into furniture or buildings.

However, psychologists know that the way we perceive the world is a complex interaction between the physical information in the environment and what we have come to expect through experience. Depth perception is a good example. We use subtle cues in the environment to help us determine how far away an object is. As you will see in this activity, our perception of distance is influenced by how large an object appears in relation to its setting, because in general, objects that appear to be large are closer than objects that appear to be small.

TIPS

- Look at the photograph of the houses in the middle of this activity. The image of the flowers in the foreground is much larger than that of the houses in the background. Yet we still perceive the houses as larger (but farther away) than the flowers. One cue that we use to help us make this judgment is the amount of detail. Close objects like the flowers are generally crisper and more detailed than objects that are farther away.

- Repeat the size-judgment task a second time while trying to ignore the background as much as possible. Were you more or less accurate when you ignored the background?

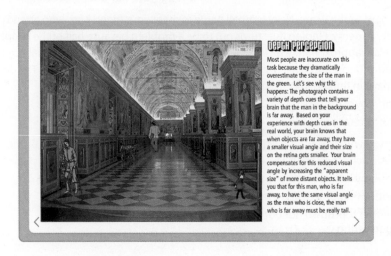

Depth Perception

Most people are inaccurate on this task because they dramatically overestimate the size of the man in the green. Let's see why this happens: The photograph contains a variety of depth cues that tell your brain that the man in the background is far away. Based on your experience with depth cues in the real world, your brain knows that when objects are far away, they have a smaller visual angle and their size on the retina gets smaller. Your brain compensates for this reduced visual angle by increasing the "apparent size" of more distant objects. It tells you that for this man, who is far away, to have the same visual angle as the man who is close, the man who is far away must be really tall.

Don't peek at the second paragraph until you answer the following questions! When held at arm's length, how large of an item (choose from a BB, a pea, a dime, a penny, a nickel, a quarter, a golf ball, a baseball, a softball, a salad plate, a Frisbee, a basketball, or a beach ball) do you think is needed to cover the moon when

- the moon is on the horizon?
- the moon is at its zenith (high in the sky)?

The answer for both is the pea, although most people will choose a larger item for the horizon than for the zenith. Based on what you have learned in the activity about depth cues that reside in our environment, why do you think this is?

MULTIPLE-CHOICE ITEMS

1. The ability to perceive depth
   a. is based solely on genetic predispositions.
   b. is, in part, learned from world experiences.
   c. is identical for all humans.
   d. exists only in humans.

2. The retina is a two-dimensional surface and therefore can represent visual stimuli in only two dimensions. Which two dimensions does the retina easily represent?
   a. height and width
   b. height and depth
   c. depth and width
   d. It can represent any two of the three dimensions, depending on the environment.

3. When Billy flips a coin, it appears to be different shapes as it rotates in the air. Sometimes it looks like a circle, sometimes like an oval, and when flat, like a thin sliver. By using which perceptual rule does Billy know that although his perception of the penny's shape may change, it never actually changes shape?
   a. relative motion   c. continuity
   b. figure and ground   d. constancy

4. Based on our experiences, our brain understands that objects far away
   a. appear larger than objects nearby.
   b. appear brighter than objects nearby.
   c. appear smaller than objects nearby.
   d. appear coarser than objects nearby.

5. Perception involves the brain
   a. ignoring cues in the environment when making judgments about size and depth.
   b. reproducing exactly the visual stimuli encountered in the environment.
   c. detecting the presence of visual stimuli.
   d. interpreting visual stimuli based on experience in the real world.

4.7 Visual Illusions

http://dragon.uml.edu/psych/illusion.html

http://www.brl.ntt.co.jp/IllusionForum/basics/visual/index-e.html

The Web sites listed above are just a few of the free visual-illusions sites available online. Simply defined, a visual illusion is a sensory display that people tend to perceive incorrectly. Although it is easy to find examples of visual illusions, cognitive psychologists have had great difficulty explaining why particular visual illusions are experienced and why many of them persist even after the viewer knows what he or she is really looking at. You may ask yourselves why cognitive psychologists would spend time trying to explain visual illusions, however intriguing they may be. Cognitive psychologists believe that visual illusions generally occur because the images violate the rules that we use to perceive the world. If we can understand why we see particular images as visual illusions, we can learn more about the rules that our perceptual system uses to make sense of the world.

T I P S

- Don't be alarmed if you do not understand the explanations given for some of the illusions on these Web sites. Cognitive psychologists have had great difficulty explaining these illusions, so it is not surprising that you might struggle as well.

- Interestingly, culture influences the perception of some visual illusions. Find the Müller-Lyer illusion online or in your textbook. People raised in cultures that do not have buildings built in square or rectangular shapes are much less likely to perceive this illusion the way you probably do.

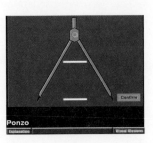  

REFLECTION QUESTION

When it comes to illusions, vision is king and the other sensory modalities lag far behind. In other words, the number of visual illusions that have been identified is much larger than the corresponding number for hearing, touch, or taste. Visual illusions have also been the subject of much more psychological research. Why do you think visual illusions receive much more attention than other kinds of illusions? Is it because our visual system processes information differently? Does it say something about the extent to which we rely on vision more than we rely on our other senses?

MULTIPLE-CHOICE ITEMS

1. Kanizsa's triangle (http://www.brl.ntt.co.jp/IllusionForum/basics/visual/index-e.html) is an example of a
   a. brightness illusion.
   b. color illusion.
   c. motion illusion.
   d. subjective contour illusion.

2. Most visual illusions
   a. are well understood by cognitive psychologists.
   b. are the result of tricks rather than true illusions.
   c. have little scientific value.
   d. have the potential to reveal the rules by which we perceive the world.

3. The color afterimage illusion (http://www.brl.ntt.co.jp/IllusionForum/basics/visual/english/SZ.01.html) demonstrates that the cones in our visual system
   a. cannot distinguish between black and white.
   b. are more attuned to motion than color.
   c. are organized as opposing "teams" (e.g., red–green).
   d. are not designed to detect subtle changes in color.

4. The horizontal-vertical illusion (http://dragon.uml.edu/psych/compact_hor_vert.html) refers to the fact that if one sees a vertical line and a horizontal line that are the same length,
   a. the vertical lines will appear to be longer than the horizontal line.
   b. the horizontal line will appear to be longer than the vertical line.
   c. the vertical line will appear to be shifted at an angle.
   d. the horizontal line will appear to be shifted at an angle.

CHAPTER FIVE

States of Consciousness

5.1 REM Sleep: Thinking

Sleep is generally viewed as a restorative phenomenon. We go to sleep physically tired and mentally groggy. We awake physically refreshed and mentally sharp. Because sleep seems to restore us both physically and mentally, we might think that our brains are as inactive during sleep as our bodies are. In fact, this is not the case. Our brains remain very active during sleep, with neural signals cascading through all portions of the brain. One stage of sleep has been of particular interest to scientists: rapid eye movement (REM) sleep. Occurring in bursts throughout the night, REM sleep is associated with heightened neural activity and vivid dreaming. Recent research has shown that REM sleep also plays an important role in learning and memory. The video you are about to watch will illustrate several research projects that have investigated the function that REM sleep serves for helping us learn from the previous day's experiences.

TIPS

- The first study in this video uses a cognitive phenomenon called *priming*. As the video describes, priming occurs when one stimulus helps facilitate the cognitive processing of a second stimulus. Priming is used in many cognitive psychology studies.

- The study on logical reasoning and REM sleep used three different control groups: those who were denied REM sleep, those who were denied sleep during other stages of sleep, and those who were allowed to sleep naturally. Think about why each of these groups was necessary. What kinds of additional measures might you take to help you compare the sleep and cognitive behavior of these three groups of subjects?

 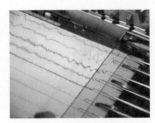 

REFLECTION QUESTIONS

1. In the video, Carlyle Smith argues that dreaming and REM sleep serve a cognitive purpose. They help us master complex reasoning tasks, although they do not seem to affect simpler memory tasks. Given this reasoning, do you think that dreaming is uniquely human? If not, what purpose do you think REM sleep and dreaming might serve in less intelligent animals?

2. What would Sigmund Freud say in response to Dr. Stickgold's claim that the content of dreams is too bizarre to arise from any kind of logical thought? What would his counter-argument be?

MULTIPLE-CHOICE ITEMS

1. According to the video, eye movements during sleep
   a. increase during times of high cognitive activity.
   b. decrease during times of high cognitive activity.
   c. are associated with dreaming but only during periods of high cognitive activity.
   d. are associated with dreaming but only during periods of low cognitive activity.

2. Priming—subconsciously recognizing the association between two related words—
   a. is higher during non-REM sleep than during REM sleep.
   b. is higher during REM sleep than during non-REM sleep.
   c. is higher while awake than during REM sleep.
   d. is unaffected by the type of sleep.

3. In one experiment, Alan Alda was awoken twice during the night—once while he was in REM sleep and once while he was not. In this experiment,
   a. performance during REM sleep was the control condition and performance during non-REM sleep was the experimental condition.
   b. performance during REM sleep was the experimental condition and performance during non-REM sleep was the control condition.
   c. performance during REM sleep and during non-REM sleep were both experimental conditions.
   d. performance during REM sleep and during non-REM sleep were both control conditions.

4. Dr. Stickgold believes that dreams are the result of the brain's attempt to make sense out of random patterns of neural signals because
   a. psychodynamic principles proved that this hypothesis was true.
   b. upon careful reflection, dreams often make more sense later than they do when initially experienced.
   c. dream content is too bizarre to be explained any other way.
   d. dream content occasionally predicts events that will occur in the future.

5. Hearing a clock tick while learning a complex reasoning task and then again while in REM sleep
   a. improved performance on a subsequent reasoning task because the clock's ticking helped the subjects focus while initially learning the task.
   b. improved performance on a subsequent reasoning task because the clock's ticking helped the subjects get more REM sleep.
   c. improved performance because the clock's ticking during REM sleep reminded the subjects of the reasoning task.
   d. hurt performance on the reasoning task because the clock's ticking interrupted REM sleep.

5.2 REM Sleep: Dreaming

Cognitive psychologists now believe that a great deal of cognitive activity occurs during REM sleep. This conclusion would have come as no surprise to Freud, who also believed that a great deal of cognitive activity occurred during REM sleep. However, whereas modern cognitive psychologists believe that REM sleep helps us learn from previous experience (see Activity 5.1, "REM Sleep: Thinking"), Freud believed that the cognitive activity that occurred during REM sleep helped conceal important psychodynamic conflicts that would otherwise disturb a peaceful night's sleep. As this video describes, Freud likened the dreams that occurred during REM sleep to a letter to oneself. If interpreted correctly, these dreams could reveal important information about the psychological struggles a person was facing. The key to accurate dream interpretation was to understand all of the cognitive work that transforms the hidden psychodynamic content of a dream into the literal content that we experience and often recall the next morning. This video will highlight some of the major themes from Freud's foundational work *The Interpretation of Dreams*.

TIPS

- Many people do not give much weight to Freud's theories because they are difficult to test empirically in controlled lab settings. As you watch the video, think about whether this criticism is fair. How might you test some of these ideas in a psychological laboratory? What barriers would prevent you from conducting such an experiment?

- The example at the end of this video might be somewhat confusing. Freud did not believe that dreams were prophetic, as you might believe from the dream described by the man at the end of the video. Still, it might be worth thinking about how the Freudian principle discussed at the beginning of the video might influence the dream described at the end. What underlying conflicts might be masked by this dream?

REFLECTION QUESTION

What kind of scientific experiment would let you evaluate any part of Freud's theory about the significance of dreaming? If you cannot devise such an experiment, what does it tell us about the viability of Freud's theory? Does it mean his theory is necessarily wrong?

MULTIPLE-CHOICE ITEMS

1. According to Freud, dreamwork
   a. served to conceal the true significance of our dreams.
   b. turned the random neural firings of our brains into a coherent, though perhaps fanciful, story.
   c. was typically observed only in the most mentally disturbed individuals.
   d. rendered the true meaning of dreams uninterpretable to both the subject and the therapist.

2. George is very angry with his mother's repeated attempts to stifle his independence. At night, George has a dream in which he repeatedly uses a catapult to hurl boulders at a castle, eventually smashing the castle to little bits. Freud might argue that in his dream, George directed his anger against the castle rather than against his mother. Freud would consider this an example of
   a. condensation.   b. symbolization.   c. displacement.   d. projection.

3. According to Freud, the *manifest* content of a dream
   a. is readily apparent to the dreamer.
   b. can be understood only with the help of a trained psychoanalyst.
   c. typically is unrelated to psychodynamic conflict.
   d. All of the above.

4. According to Freud, the *latent* content of a dream
   a. is readily apparent to the dreamer.
   b. can be understood only with the help of a trained psychoanalyst.
   c. typically is unrelated to psychodynamic conflict.
   d. All of the above.

5. Many of the dreams that were the subject of Freud's masterwork *The Interpretation of Dreams* dealt with themes related to
   a. homosexuality.
   b. loss.
   c. the Oedipus complex.
   d. toilet training and other aspects of infant development.

5.3 Drug Effects

Many common drugs, including alcohol, nicotine, and caffeine, are *psychoactive drugs*. Psychoactive drugs affect the way neurons communicate with one another. As you would expect, psychoactive drugs can either increase or decrease the likelihood that the postsynaptic neuron will send an action potential. But there are various ways that these effects can take place. Drugs can affect either

- the amount of neurotransmitter released by the presynaptic neuron.
- the rate at which released neurotransmitters are reabsorbed or removed from the synapse.
- the ability of the neurotransmitter to bind with the postsynaptic neuron.

This activity will demonstrate the ways that specific drugs affect synaptic communication. The drug effects listed are only a few examples of the ways that psychoactive drugs function. There are many other ways psychoactive drugs can affect brain activity.

TIPS

- Try to place each example in one of the three categories of drug effects listed above.
- Keep in mind that for each type of effect demonstrated in this activity, there are other drugs that have the opposite effect. For example, some drugs increase the amount of neurotransmitter released by the presynaptic synapse, which increases the firing of the postsynaptic neuron. Other drugs decrease the amount of neurotransmitter released by the presynaptic neuron, which decreases the firing of the postsynaptic neuron.

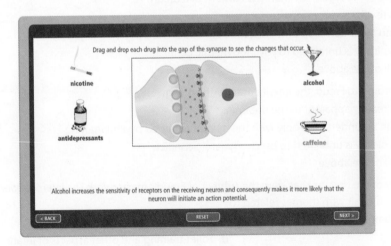

REFLECTION QUESTIONS

1. After a hard day at work, John decides to go to a local bar to unwind. While at the bar, he has a few beers and smokes a few cigarettes. What is happening to him neurologically? As the evening winds down, John decides to have a large cup of coffee before heading home. Now what is happening to John neurologically?

2. You are working on an antidrug campaign. You have to produce a thirty-second public-service announcement discussing the effects of drugs on neural activity. What are you going to say? (Remember to communicate the information in an understandable way to all people.)

MULTIPLE-CHOICE ITEMS

1. Communication *between* neurons involves which activity?
   a. Neurotransmitters are released by the sending neuron into the synapse and stimulate receptors on the receiving neuron.
   b. Action potential crosses the synapse from the sending neuron to the receiving neuron.
   c. Neurotransmitters exit the dendrites of the sending neuron and attach to the axons of the receiving neuron.
   d. The receptors of the receiving neurons attach to the axon of the sending neuron, allowing neurotransmitters to travel across neurons.

2. After several weeks of taking the antidepressant Zoloft, Stefanie begins to feel less depressed. The neural activity responsible for the elevation in Stefanie's mood involves
   a. an increase in the breakdown of neurotransmitters remaining in the synapse after neural firing.
   b. a reduction in the stimulation of the receiving neuron after the sending neuron fires.
   c. a reduction of neurotransmitters in the synapse after the sending neuron fires.
   d. an increase of neurotransmitters in the synapse after the sending neuron fires.

3. After drinking a few glasses of wine,
   a. the sensitivity of receptors on receiving neurons is increased.
   b. the sensitivity of receptors on receiving neurons is decreased.
   c. the amount of neurotransmitters released into the synapse is increased.
   d. the amount of neurotransmitters released into the synapse is decreased.

4. Tammy loves coffee and has several cups a day. Neurologically, how is the caffeine affecting Tammy?
   a. The amount of neurotransmitters released into the synapse is increased.
   b. The likelihood of the receiving neurons' firing is increased.
   c. Both a and b
   d. Neither a nor b

5. The effects of psychoactive drugs on neural communication

   a. are to always slow down neural activity.

   b. vary depending on the type of drug ingested.

   c. affect only the amount of neurotransmitters in the synapse but not the receiving neuron's sensitivity.

   d. affect only the receiving neuron's sensitivity but not the amount of the neurotransmitters in the synapse.

5.4 Hypnosis

Ellen tried to quit smoking several times. She tried gums, patches, and support groups, but nothing worked for very long. She did manage to quit while she was pregnant, but then she started smoking (outside of the house when her child was not around) soon after giving birth. In desperation, she tried hypnosis. It worked. Ellen never smoked another cigarette, even though there were times when she desperately wanted one. There are many case studies like Ellen's in which hypnotic states lead to powerful behavioral breakthroughs. In addition to smoking cessation, hypnosis is used to help cure phobias, gain access to repressed childhood memories, help flesh out crime witnesses' memories, and alleviate the pain associated with certain medical procedures. Despite ample evidence of the positive effects of hypnosis, the scientific community has had great difficulty validating these effects scientifically. The article that you will read provides an overview of the claims made by those who believe that hypnotic states are associated with powerful possibilities, as well as counterarguments made by those skeptical of the power of hypnosis.

TIPS

- Do case studies, like the fictional case of Ellen above, sufficiently prove that hypnosis works? Some people quoted in the article think they do, whereas others will disagree. Think about the evidence presented on both sides before drawing your own conclusions.

- Some would argue that scientific principles cannot be used to evaluate transcendent states of consciousness like hypnosis or ESP. A broader issue concerns the appropriateness of using science to study human behavior. Do you think that science is always the best way to study human behavior?

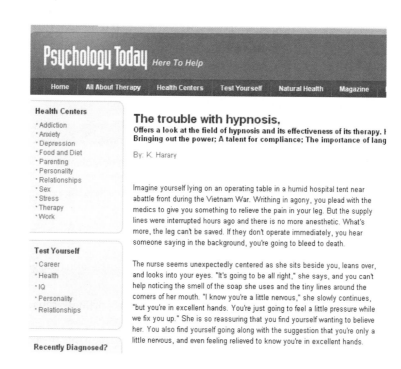

Psychology Today Here To Help

| Home | All About Therapy | Health Centers | Test Yourself | Natural Health | Magazine |

Health Centers

- Addiction
- Anxiety
- Depression
- Food and Diet
- Parenting
- Personality
- Relationships
- Sex
- Stress
- Therapy
- Work

Test Yourself

- Career
- Health
- IQ
- Personality
- Relationships

Recently Diagnosed?

The trouble with hypnosis.

Offers a look at the field of hypnosis and its effectiveness of its therapy. I
Bringing out the power; A talent for compliance; The importance of lang

By: K. Harary

Imagine yourself lying on an operating table in a humid hospital tent near a battle front during the Vietnam War. Writhing in agony, you plead with the medics to give you something to relieve the pain in your leg. But the supply lines were interrupted hours ago and there is no more anesthetic. What's more, the leg can't be saved. If they don't operate immediately, you hear someone saying in the background, you're going to bleed to death.

The nurse seems unexpectedly centered as she sits beside you, leans over, and looks into your eyes. "It's going to be all right," she says, and you can't help noticing the smell of the soap she uses and the tiny lines around the corners of her mouth. "I know you're a little nervous," she slowly continues, "but you're in excellent hands. You're just going to feel a little pressure while we fix you up." She is so reassuring that you find yourself wanting to believe her. You also find yourself going along with the suggestion that you're only a little nervous, and even feeling relieved to know you're in excellent hands.

REFLECTION QUESTION

According to the article that you read, psychologists have yet to identify a specific pattern of neural activity that reliably signals when someone has entered a hypnotic state. Is this conclusive evidence that hypnosis does not produce a distinct mental state? How might a true believer in hypnosis explain this failure?

MULTIPLE-CHOICE ITEMS

1. Which of the following statements about a person's susceptibility to hypnosis is true?
   a. People vary in their susceptibility to hypnosis.
   b. Susceptibility to hypnosis appears to be stable within an individual over long time periods.
   c. Both a and b
   d. Neither a nor b

2. Using hypnosis for therapeutic purposes
   a. began in the last half century.
   b. began at the dawn of the twentieth century, around the time of Freud.
   c. began approximately two centuries ago.
   d. began in ancient Greece.

3. According to the article, which of the following represents a current or past application of hypnosis?
   a. to remove warts without the use of any medical procedures
   b. to eliminate pain during open-heart surgery
   c. to help people locate misplaced valuables like jewelry
   d. to help people prepare for Introductory Psychology exams

4. The scientific study of hypnosis is plagued by the fact that
   a. there is an objective procedure for inducing hypnosis but no objective procedure for determining whether a subject has been hypnotized.
   b. there is an objective procedure for determining whether a subject has been hypnotized but no objective procedure for inducing hypnosis.
   c. several objective procedures for inducing hypnosis exist, but no consensus exists as to which procedure is best.
   d. there is no objective procedure for inducing hypnosis or for determining whether a subject has been hypnotized.

5. Which of the following constitutes evidence that the effects of hypnosis can be attributed to the suggestibility of subjects?
   a. People show the same likelihood of responding to a suggestion that their arm feels very heavy whether or not they have been hypnotized.
   b. Susceptibility to hypnosis appears to be stable within an individual over long time periods.
   c. Hypnosis has been effective in helping reduce the experience of pain during childbirth.
   d. Hypnosis has been effective in reducing phobias like fear of flying.

Learning

6.1 Classical Conditioning: Pavlov's Dogs

Classical conditioning is an elementary component of the modern understanding of how organisms—including human beings—learn. The concept that is most central to your understanding of classical conditioning is *association*. Association refers to the extent to which two stimuli tend to co-occur in the environment (you could think of this as a correlation between two stimuli). The strength of an association is governed by many factors, including:

- *Frequency of exposure:* The more often two stimuli tend to co-occur, the stronger the association between these stimuli will become. If your friend never cleans his room, you will come to associate his room with disgust.

- *Temporal contiguity:* The more closely two stimuli occur in time, the stronger the association will be. The pain that comes from stubbing your toe follows very quickly after experiencing the event.

- *Intensity:* Associations will be formed more strongly for emotionally intense experiences than for more neutral ones. Taste aversions can be formed by a single exposure to a food that makes us ill.

These activities will trace the history of classical conditioning back to Ivan Pavlov's pioneering work with salivating dogs. They will also introduce a number of vocabulary terms related to the study of classical conditioning and explain how associations are formed and subsequently lost. They will also demonstrate how classical conditioning can be observed in situations that you might encounter every day.

TIPS

- Think about how frequency of exposure, temporal contiguity, and intensity operate in both the acquisition and the extinction phases of the activities.

- Decide whether it is possible to model the effects of these variables in these activities. If not, think about how you might modify the program to show these effects.

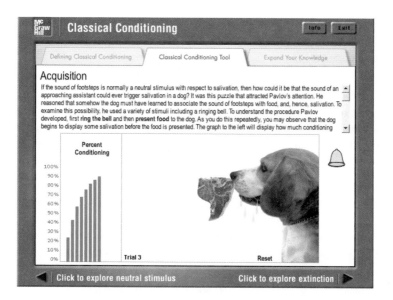

Acquisition

If the sound of footsteps is normally a neutral stimulus with respect to salivation, then how could it be that the sound of an approaching assistant could ever trigger salivation in a dog? It was this puzzle that attracted Pavlov's attention. He reasoned that somehow the dog must have learned to associate the sound of footsteps with food, and, hence, salivation. To examine this possibility, he used a variety of stimuli including a ringing bell. To understand the procedure Pavlov developed, first **ring the bell** and then **present food** to the dog. As you do this repeatedly, you may observe that the dog begins to display some salivation before the food is presented. The graph to the left will display how much conditioning

REFLECTION QUESTIONS

1. Pets often demonstrate the best examples of classical conditioning by learning very quickly to associate new stimuli with old stimuli–response relationships. Describe an example of how a pet might be classically conditioned to salivate to the sound of a can opener. Now give examples of how the pet might generalize this salivation response (again using the can opener). Finally, what might be a way to extinguish salivating to the sound of a can opener?

2. Food aversions are often classically conditioned in just one trial. That is, when a person is exposed to a food and then gets sick, that person is likely to always feel nauseated in the presence of that specific food. Can you think of a particular food or drink to which you have been classically conditioned to feel nauseated? Describe the experience. Has this aversion generalized to other foods? Describe.

MULTIPLE-CHOICE ITEMS

Laurie walks home from work every day and has been doing so happily for years. One evening, as Laurie is walking down Pace Street, a mugger grabs her from behind and takes her bag, leaving Laurie very frightened. Now, every time Laurie finds herself walking on Pace Street, she becomes fearful, even though the mugger has been put behind bars.

1. In this example, the unconditioned reflex (the UCS → UCR) is
   a. mugging → fear response.
   b. walking on Pace Street → fear response.
   c. fear response → mugging.
   d. fear response → walking on Pace Street.

2. Laurie's current fearfulness when walking on Pace Street can best be described as the
   a. unconditioned stimulus.
   c. conditioned stimulus.
   b. unconditioned response.
   d. conditioned response.

3. For six months, Matt has put on his green coat whenever he is getting ready to walk his dog, Peach. Whenever Peach sees Matt put on his green coat, Peach jumps up and down wildly with excitement. Matt received a brown coat for his birthday and decided to put it on to walk Peach. When he donned his coat, however, Peach did not jump up and down as she usually does. Peach's lack of excitement about going on a walk is most likely due to
   a. extinction.
   c. discrimination.
   b. generalization.
   d. habituation.

4. When the bell rings at the end of a class, Sheila knows to put her books away. One day, Sheila is in the library reading a book and her friend's cell phone begins to ring. Immediately, even though she is planning on staying at the library for another hour, Sheila begins to put her book in her backpack. Sheila's behavior appears to be a result of
   a. discrimination.
   c. habituation.
   b. generalization.
   d. spontaneous recovery.

5. Mark moved to an apartment that is very close to the train station. At first, each time a train would pass his apartment in the middle of the night, the noise would wake Mark up abruptly. After a few weeks, however, Mark began to sleep through the night and now is never disturbed by a passing train. Mark's behavior appears to be the result of
   a. discrimination.
   c. habituation.
   b. generalization.
   d. spontaneous recovery.

6.2 Classical Conditioning and Advertising

Classical conditioning is an elementary form of learning. An organism learns to associate a new response to a stimulus because that stimulus has co-occurred with some other stimulus in the past. That may seem a confusing definition, but classical conditioning is really rather easy to understand. The "classic" example of classical conditioning is that of Pavlov's dogs. Pavlov was studying the physiology of salivary glands in dogs. He noticed that his research subjects learned to salivate whenever one of his research assistants approached the dogs. How did Pavlov explain this observation? He hypothesized that the dogs learned to associate the research assistants with the food that they often brought with them. Therefore, they learned to salivate in response to the research assistants' approach because it frequently co-occurred with food.

This activity begins with a brief overview of the experiments that Pavlov used to confirm his hypothesis. Classical conditioning is not limited to dogs; there are many everyday examples of classical conditioning with humans. Advertising campaigns are perhaps the most prevalent overt attempts to train people using classical conditioning. This activity will demonstrate how the principles of classical conditioning have been used in political advertisements to sway voters' opinions.

- Think about how each of the three ads used classical conditioning to sell their message. Which do you think was most effective? Do you think that your political views influenced your assessment of the ads? Ask your parents or grandparents if they remember the Goldwater/atom bomb ad that you saw. Do they recall the ad? Did it affect the way they voted or their political views?

- The power of classical conditioning is determined in large measure by the number of exposures that the subject has to the to-be-learned stimulus. Pavlov's dogs received many exposures to the research assistants' bringing them food. But advertisers cannot necessarily count on your seeing their ads multiple times. That is why new ad campaigns often flood the media, competing for our time and attention.

- Another important thing to note is that advertisers often try to use covert means to form classically conditioned associations. This is different from Pavlov's overt combination of bells and food. Think about how using covert associations might affect how strongly these associations are formed.

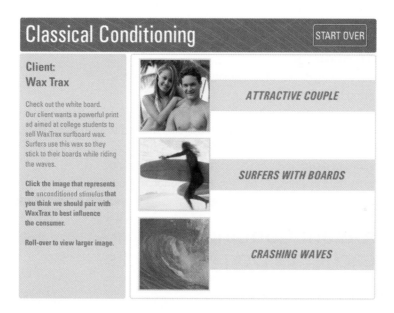

REFLECTION QUESTION

Advertisers have been using the principles of classical conditioning for years in attempts to associate pleasant feelings with their products. Beer ads are particularly famous for doing so by placing scantily clothed women holding beer bottles on large billboards. What are the unconditioned stimulus and the unconditioned response in this example? What are the conditioned stimulus and conditioned response?

Jillian, a stay-at-home mother, watches a lot of daytime television. During the day, Charmin toilet paper runs lots of television ads. Jillian always smiles when she sees these ads because they feature cute babies. When Jillian is shopping at her local market, she finds herself smiling when she is in the toilet-paper section, especially when she is near the Charmin toilet paper.

1. In this example, the unconditioned stimulus(i) is (are) the
   a. toilet paper.   b. cute babies.   c. television.   d. local market.

2. Jillian's smiling at the cute babies is a(n)
   a. unconditioned stimulus.   c. conditioned stimulus.
   b. unconditioned response.   d. conditioned response.

3. _____ is the conditioned stimulus and _____ is the conditioned response in the above example.
   a. Cute babies; smiling   c. Cute babies; shopping
   b. Toilet paper; shopping   d. Toilet paper; smiling

4. Laura watched a public-service announcement to curb smoking in which a young boy described how his mother died from lung cancer after smoking for twenty years. In this example, the unconditioned response would be
   a. sadness regarding a mother's death.
   b. fear of smoking.
   c. contracting lung cancer after smoking for twenty years.
   d. the young boy's story.

5. When Tobias passed his driver's exam, the song "Fire and Rain" by James Taylor was playing on the radio. Now, whenever Tobias hears this sad song, he feels joyous. Tobias's joyful reaction to the sad song can be classified as a(n)
   a. unconditioned stimulus.   c. conditioned stimulus.
   b. unconditioned response.   d. conditioned response.

6.3 Operant Conditioning: Teaching a Dog New Tricks

Operant conditioning is similar to classical conditioning in that both are models of how organisms learn about their environment. However, the two forms of learning differ in several ways. Classical conditioning generally involves transferring a behavior that an animal already does (e.g., salivating in response to food) to a new stimulus (e.g., salivating in response to a bell or footsteps). Operant conditioning is broader in that virtually any behavior can be trained via operant conditioning if the animal receives the right kind of *reinforcement*. Reinforcement is something that an animal receives for performing some form of behavior. As the video in this activity demonstrates, reinforcement can take the form of a reward, like praise or a gift for a job well done. But it can also take the form of punishment, like being grounded for getting a bad grade. Although this video focuses on training a dog to do tricks, it is important to note that evidence of operant conditioning can be found in many of the daily tasks we do.

- The video demonstrates another important difference between operant and classical conditioning. Operant conditioning can be used to discourage an animal from engaging in a specific behavior. This is not to say that classically conditioned responses cannot be extinguished: they can, but only after they have been acquired.

- Also note that operant conditioning can be used to teach an animal complex, multistep behaviors. Later, in Activity 6.5 ("Shaping"), you will have an opportunity to teach a virtual pet bird a complex behavior using operant conditioning.

REFLECTION QUESTION

Susie, Sally, and Serena are roommates. Susie and Sally are neat freaks, but Serena is a slob. Both Susie and Sally want to use reinforcement to get Serena to start picking up her messes. Susie wants to use positive reinforcement as her technique, and Sally wants to use negative reinforcement. Devise a plan for Susie and another for Sally based on each person's reinforcement style.

MULTIPLE-CHOICE ITEMS

1. Every time Susan gets an A on her report card, her father gives her $10. Susan's dad is using _____ to encourage her to continue to do well in school.
   a. positive reinforcement   c. primary reinforcement
   b. negative reinforcement   d. discriminatory reinforcement

2. Every time Bill gets an A on his report card, his father removes one of the tasks from Bill's list of weekly chores. Bill's dad is using _____ to encourage him to continue to do well in school.
   a. positive reinforcement   c. primary reinforcement
   b. negative reinforcement   d. discriminatory reinforcement

3. Whenever little Jake hits his sister Abby, Jake's mom takes away one of his toys. Jake's mom is using which operant-conditioning technique?
   a. negative reinforcement
   b. shaping
   c. punishment
   d. discriminatory reinforcement

4. Food is a _____ reinforcer; money is a _____ reinforcer.
   a. primary; primary
   b. primary; secondary
   c. secondary; primary
   d. secondary; secondary

5. Greg is teaching Billy to juggle. First Greg praises Billy for tossing and catching one ball at a time; next Greg praises Billy for tossing and catching two balls at a time; finally, Greg praises Billy for tossing and catching three balls at a time. Greg is relying on which operant-conditioning technique?
   a. cue discrimination
   b. primary reinforcers
   c. reflexive training
   d. shaping

6.4 Reinforcement and Punishment

According to B. F. Skinner, all learning—whether by one-celled animals or *Homo sapiens*—is achieved via rewards (which he called *reinforcement*) and punishment. Reinforcement makes it more likely that we will engage in some behavior. Punishment makes it less likely that we will engage in some behavior. Both reinforcement and punishment can be achieved by adding a stimulus or taking a stimulus away. Thus, according to Skinner, there are four ways to influence learning:

- *Positive reinforcement:* giving something pleasant to encourage a behavior (e.g., paying a teenager for completing her paper route)

- *Negative reinforcement:* taking away something pleasant to encourage a behavior (e.g., grounding a teenager for not completing her paper route)

- *Positive punishment:* giving something positive to discourage a behavior (e.g., offering a toddler some candy if he stops fidgeting during his haircut)

- *Negative punishment:* taking away something negative to discourage a behavior (e.g., promising that you will stop yelling at a toddler if he stops fidgeting during his haircut)

This activity will give you an opportunity to experience different kinds of punishment and reinforcement in a restaurant setting. Your job will be to deliver food to the right tables. You will be rewarded with positive and negative reinforcement if you do so efficiently and will receive negative punishment if you do not.

TIPS

- It is not too difficult to navigate an entire shift without making any mistakes. If you must prove this to yourself, go ahead and do so. Either way, run through the program once while allowing yourself to make mistakes so that you can see the effect of punishment.

- At the end of the activity, you are asked which form of reinforcement or punishment was most effective in shaping your behavior in this activity. Do you think that this means of motivation is most effective in other situations as well? What is it about this restaurant game that made this particular form of punishment/reinforcement so effective?

REFLECTION QUESTION

You have just been hired as a babysitter for the Old Woman Who Lived in a Shoe's fifteen children. As the old woman leaves for a night on the town, she tells you that she has three rules regarding the children's playtime: (1) they can play with whatever toys they want, but they have to clean their playroom before bedtime; (2) they should share their toys with each other; and (3) they are not allowed to fight with each other. Using the principles of reinforcement and punishment, devise a strategy to fulfill her three requirements.

MULTIPLE-CHOICE ITEMS

1. Julie works at a factory that produces toy clowns. As the toy clowns come down the assembly line, it is Julie's job to add a red nose to each clown as the last step in completing each toy. For every 100 clowns Kelly completes, she receives $10.00, which is a(n)

   a. primary reinforcement.
   c. positive reinforcement.

   b. incentive reinforcement.
   d. negative reinforcement.

2. To increase productivity, the clown factory decides to have a contest. The person who completes the most clowns on Monday does not have to come to work on Tuesday. The factory is using _____ as a motivator.
   a. positive reinforcement
   b. negative reinforcement
   c. primary reinforcement
   d. discriminatory reinforcement

3. The clown factory's bosses do not like laziness. If a worker completes fewer than twenty toys during the morning hours, they do not get to take a lunch break. This behavioral tactic is an example of
   a. negative reinforcement.
   b. positive reinforcement.
   c. positive punishment.
   d. negative punishment.

4. The clown factory's bosses also do not like mistakes. If a worker forgets to put a nose on a clown, the bosses publicly scold the worker. This behavioral tactic is an example of
   a. negative reinforcement.
   b. positive reinforcement.
   c. positive punishment.
   d. negative punishment.

5. As you can see from the examples above, the clown factory's bosses use _____ to increase behaviors they like and _____ to decrease behaviors they do not like.
   a. positive reinforcement; negative reinforcement
   b. primary reinforcement; secondary reinforcement
   c. positive punishment; negative punishment
   d. reinforcement; punishment

6.5 Shaping

If you have ever had a dog, you have probably experienced operant conditioning first-hand. Think about when you housebroke your dog: How did you do it? You probably took the dog outside and waited for Fluffy to do her business. Then you praised her lavishly or gave her a dog treat. With more and more practice, Fluffy learned to associate doing her business outside with earning some sort of reward, which increased the likelihood of her engaging in that behavior outside in the future.

Shaping is a form of operant conditioning used to train animals to perform more complex tasks. The task is broken down into a series of smaller, simpler tasks, and the animal is rewarded for each step along the way until the final complex behavior is accomplished. For example, dolphins at a marine park might be trained to wave at a crowd with their tails. This complex behavior might be accomplished by rewarding the dolphin first for swimming to the side of the pool. After this step has been mastered, the dolphin might be rewarded for swimming to the side of the pool *and* turning upside down; then for swimming to the side of the pool, turning upside down, *and* sticking its tail out of the water; then for swimming to the side of the pool, turning upside down, sticking its tail out of the water, *and* moving its tail back and forth.

It's important to note that humans are also susceptible to shaping and operant conditioning. Ask your parents how they "housebroke" you. The story you hear will probably remind you a lot of Fluffy, although most of the drama probably took place inside rather than outside. In this activity, you will have the opportunity to shape the behavior of a virtual pet: you will teach Jingles the parakeet to ring a bell.

TIPS

- Timing is everything with shaping; be sure to reward Jingles as soon as her behavior changes in the desired direction.
- Don't reward Jingles twice for the same behavior, or it will be difficult to lead her to the next step.
- After you successfully shape Jingles once, rerun the simulation, but reward her periodically regardless of what she does. Notice how her behavior becomes random rather than goal-directed.

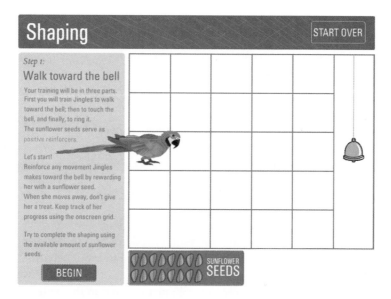

REFLECTION QUESTION

Suppose you were in charge of toilet training your 2-year-old sister. Set up a reinforcement system using the operant-conditioning method of shaping. What steps toward the goal would you reinforce? What reinforcer do you think would be most effective?

MULTIPLE-CHOICE QUESTIONS

1. Matt is trying to teach his dog Peach how to roll over. He first gives Peach a treat whenever Peach sits. Next, he no longer rewards Peach for sitting but rather gives Peach a treat when the dog actually lies down. Finally, Matt rewards Peach only when the dog rolls over. Matt is using _____ to train Peach to roll over.
   a. generalization
   b. discrimination
   c. shaping
   d. extinction

2. A bird will learn very quickly to tap a lever if it is reinforced with birdseed for doing so. Birdseed is an effective reward because it is a _____ reinforcer.

   a. primary

   b. secondary

   c. neutral

   d. negative

3. If Coach Winner wants to use shaping successfully to teach Betsy Beginner how to serve a tennis ball, he should

   a. reinforce Betsy only when she can serve a ball perfectly.

   b. reinforce Betsy for correctly tossing the ball, then for correctly swinging her racket, then for correctly hitting the ball, and finally for aiming the ball into the correct box.

   c. allow Betsy to practice for a week without feedback and then evaluate her progress at the end of the week.

   d. remain neutral when providing Betsy feedback about her serve.

4. Which of the following is an example of a primary reinforcer?

   a. paying a worker $10 for cleaning the floors

   b. catching a fish and eating it

   c. giving a child a gold star for earning an A on an exam

   d. allowing a teen to stay out past curfew

5. Bob Boss rewards his telemarketers with $5 every time they make a phone call. What type of reinforcement is Bob using?

   a. negative reinforcement

   b. partial reinforcement

   c. primary reinforcement

   d. continuous reinforcement

6.6 Schedules of Reinforcement

According to Skinner, all behaviors are the result of rewards and punishment. We tend to engage in behaviors that were rewarded in the past and to avoid behaviors that were punished in the past. Another important aspect of Skinner's theory is the way rewards and punishments are experienced over time. Skinner referred to the pattern of rewards and punishments as a *schedule of reinforcement.* According to him, there were four different schedules of reinforcement: fixed interval, fixed ratio, variable interval, and variable ratio. This activity will provide definitions for each of these schedules of reinforcement. The activity will also give you an opportunity to use different schedules of reinforcement to motivate the wait staff at Café Cogito. Your goal will be to increase the productivity of the staff by tailoring the reinforcement schedule to each member of the staff.

TIPS

- Get to know each member of the staff before continuing with the activity. This information will be helpful when trying to decide which schedule of reinforcement to assign to each server.

- This activity does not take very long to complete, so it might be interesting to try different combinations of schedules and servers to see how they affect productivity.

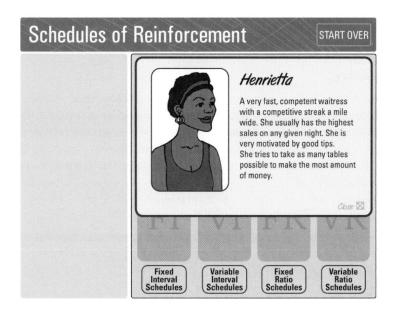

Schedules of Reinforcement — START OVER

Henrietta

A very fast, competent waitress with a competitive streak a mile wide. She usually has the highest sales on any given night. She is very motivated by good tips. She tries to take as many tables possible to make the most amount of money.

Close ⊠

| Fixed Interval Schedules | Variable Interval Schedules | Fixed Ratio Schedules | Variable Ratio Schedules |

REFLECTION QUESTION

As you have learned from the exercise, there are many ways to adjust the timing and frequency of reinforcement. Employers use a variety of these schedules of reinforcement to reward employees. For example, a toy-factory employer may use a fixed ratio schedule of reinforcement and pay an assembly line worker for every 100 toys he assembles. How might the toy-factory employer use each of the other three reinforcement schedules (variable ratio; fixed interval; variable interval) to pay her workers? Which schedule do you think will motivate the workers to produce the most toys?

MULTIPLE-CHOICE ITEMS

1. Behavior that is rewarded some but not all of the time is on a _____ schedule of reinforcement.
   a. partial
   b. intermittent
   c. continuous
   d. full

2. The _____ schedule of reinforcement reinforces behavior only after a specific number of responses are made.
   a. fixed ratio
   b. variable ratio
   c. fixed interval
   d. variable interval

3. Edwin Employer pays his workers at 5:00 PM every Friday. Edwin is using which schedule of reinforcement to reward his employees?
   a. fixed ratio
   b. variable ratio
   c. fixed interval
   d. variable interval

4. The reinforcement schedule that typically yields the highest response rate is the
_____ schedule of reinforcement.
   a. fixed ratio
   b. variable ratio
   c. fixed interval
   d. variable interval

5. Professor McMann loves to give pop quizzes in his psychology class. Students are always studying for this class because they never know when Professor McMann will give the next quiz. Sometimes he gives a pop quiz every other class session, sometimes he gives a pop quiz every third session, and sometimes he even gives a pop quiz every class session. Professor McMann is using which schedule of reinforcement to keep his students studying?
   a. fixed ratio
   b. variable ratio
   c. fixed interval
   d. variable interval

6.7 Observational Learning: Monkey See, Monkey Do

Matt is 40 years old—not terribly old, but not terribly young either. For Father's Day, his wife, Tammy, bought him an MP3 player. This turned out to be a great gift. Matt read the instructions and loaded all of his favorite music onto his MP3 player. There was only one problem. Matt could not figure how to do something that is fairly simple: he could not turn the MP3 player off. He would hit the pause button, and eventually the light would go off. Finally, Matt went to the electronics store and asked one of the clerks if there was indeed a way to turn the machine off. There was. The clerk demonstrated the buttons to press, and Matt was once again ecstatic. He could turn off his MP3 player whenever he wanted. The clerk also showed Matt where this information was located in the owner's manual. The interaction between Matt and the electronics store clerk is an example of *observational learning*. Matt watched the clerk and simply copied his behaviors.

Observational learning has been implicated in all kinds of human behaviors. For example, teenagers who smoke are very likely to have parents who smoke. Although other factors are certainly involved, some have theorized that such teenagers learn to smoke by watching their parents. Observational learning has also been implicated in domestic violence. One might ask how the strong propensity to copy the behavior of other humans has evolved. One might argue that copying the behavior of others might help transmit useful skills before language (like instruction manuals for MP3 players) developed. If this was the case, one might expect our nearest primate relatives to show similar patterns of observational learning. This video will describe some research that has examined the form that observational learning takes in primates and humans.

- Observational learning is easy to observe if you have access to a human toddler. Show the toddler a new toy. If you bounce it, the child will bounce the toy. If you throw the toy, the child will throw the toy. If you hide it under your shirt, the toddler will likely do the same. Toddlers are amazing imitating machines!

- Take special note of how Dr. Tomasello designed the human experiment to mimic the orangutan experiment as closely as possible. This is very important when designing studies to compare behavior across different species of animals. Think about whether there were ways in which the two experiments differed that might influence the results of the experiment.

- Also take special notice of how the young girl who participates in the experiment has her own ideas about the best way to retrieve the toy!

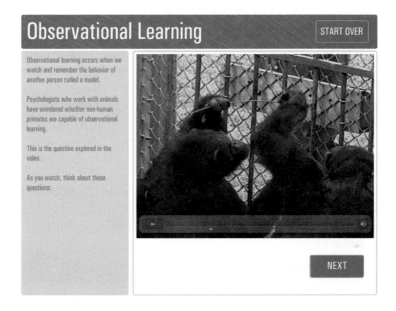

REFLECTION QUESTION

One difference between the human experiment and the orangutan experiment was that Alan Alda was capable of communicating with the humans using language. Does this difference influence the way you interpret the different kinds of behaviors exhibited by the humans and the primates?

1. According to Dr. Tomasello, one explanation for how chimpanzees learn to use a stick to "fish" for honey is that the skill is
   a. innate.
   b. the result of evolution.
   c. learned by watching their human caregivers use keys to open locks.
   d. an example of insightful problem solving by nonhuman primates.

2. The orangutans in the video
   a. failed to learn to use the rake to obtain fruit.
   b. used the rake but not in the most efficient way.
   c. were so uncooperative that it would be hard to know whether they were capable of observational learning.
   d. None of the above.

3. The video with the orangutans also showed that orangutans
   a. are capable of devising independent strategic uses for tools.
   b. learn in much the same way as humans.
   c. cannot learn from watching humans.
   d. cannot learn from watching other orangutans.

4. When comparing observational learning in humans and nonhuman primates, it appears that
   a. both humans and other primates mimic the broad outlines of a behavior but not the specific details.
   b. humans and primates are equally likely to mimic the specific details of an observed behavior.
   c. other primates are more likely than humans to mimic the specific details of an observed behavior.
   d. humans are more likely than other primates to mimic the specific details of an observed behavior.

5. At one point in this exercise Alan Alda says, "I think the reason that they don't do exactly what I do is because I don't grab it with my feet; I'm just using my hands." Imagine that we could find a talented circus performer who could manipulate the rake with his feet almost as well as the orangutans. Watching the circus performer use the rake would most likely produce which of the following results?
   a. The orangutans would be more likely to use the rake as demonstrated and would learn to imitate the skill more quickly.
   b. The orangutans would be more likely to use the rake as demonstrated, but they would not learn to imitate the skill any faster.
   c. The orangutans' behavior would not be affected.
   d. The orangutans feelings would be hurt because they would think that the circus performer was making fun of them.

CHAPTER SEVEN

Memory

7.1 Sensory Memory

One of the first questions that cognitive psychologists tried to answer is, How much information can we hold in memory at any one time? The simplest way to address this question was to present people with large arrays of letters or numbers for brief periods of time. After the arrays were removed from view, the research subjects were asked to report as many of the letters or numbers from the arrays as possible. Early work using this method suggested that people could retain three or four items in memory at once. In other words, no matter how many letters were in the array, the subjects were able to report only three or four items.

George Sperling believed that these experiments greatly underestimated the amount of information that people could hold in memory and developed an ingenious experiment to test his hypothesis. This activity will give you an opportunity to test your own memory in an online version of what has come to be known as the Sperling task.

TIPS

- Before starting this activity, turn off your cell phone, your MP3 player or stereo, and any other computer programs that are currently running on your machine, including instant messaging. This experiment requires your full attention. If you look away— even for a moment—while the letters are on the computer screen, you will lose the opportunity to experience for yourself how sensory memory works. It is not a very long experiment, so you will not be cut off from the world for more than a minute or two.

- Try to fixate on the two middle boxes in the middle row of the array. This will give you the best opportunity to simultaneously view all twelve boxes in the array.

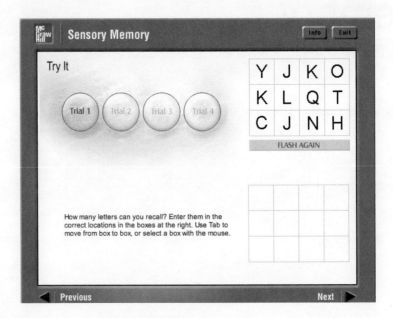

REFLECTION QUESTIONS

1. The Sperling sensory-memory studies are a good example of how several experiments are needed to draw accurate conclusions about human behavior. Sperling conducted three types of studies: whole report, partial report–immediate, and partial report–delay. What incorrect conclusion regarding the capacity of sensory memory would Sperling have made if he had conducted only the whole report study? What incorrect conclusion about the duration of sensory memory would Sperling have made if he had conducted only the partial report–immediate study?

2. Sperling's studies focused on the sense of vision. Can you generate a similar experiment using a different sense (e.g., audition, touch)? How would you design such a study?

MULTIPLE-CHOICE ITEMS

1. An example of sensory memory might be
   a. remembering the first time you tasted a lemon.
   b. remembering an episode using a particular sense such as touching a baby's soft skin.
   c. a brief memorial representation of a road sign you pass while driving.
   d. a memory based on both sound and sight.

2. In the whole report experiment, participants
   a. were unable to recall any of the letters in the matrix.
   b. were able to recall an average of four to five letters in the matrix.
   c. were able to recall three to four of the letters in the row of the matrix designated by the tone.
   d. were able to recall all of the letters in the matrix.

3. By combining data from the partial report–immediate and partial report–delay studies, Sperling concluded that
   a. the presentation of the letters in the matrix was too fast for any participant to enter them into the sensory store.
   b. if you present only a partial mix of the letters in the array, participants can recall all of them.
   c. participants can see all the letters in the matrix but the image fades after they report only a few of them.
   d. participants can see only a few of the letters in the matrix when they are flashed on a screen.

4. Sensory memory fades
   a. very fast, sometimes after less than one second.
   b. fast, after five to seven seconds.
   c. slowly, usually after twenty seconds.
   d. not at all; its resolution is thought to last infinitely.

5. Based on Sperling's sensory-memory studies, we can conclude that
   a. capacity for sensory memory is small and its duration is very short.
   b. capacity for sensory memory is quite large and its duration is very long.
   c. although sensory memory's capacity is small, its duration is very long.
   d. although sensory memory's capacity is quite large, its duration is very short.

7.2 Working Memory: Decay versus Interference

Once again, you have forgotten the password for your school's course-registration Web site. So you go to the registrar's office, and the nice folks there generate a new password for you. You are determined not to forget your password again. What could you do to help you remember it? You could write the password down, but what if your roommate found your password and, as a joke, registered you for a class that met Monday through Friday at 8:00 AM along with a physics lab and two chemistry labs?

If you are like most people, you would use the "little voice inside your head" to repeat the username and password over and over until you were sure you could remember it. *Working memory* is that "voice inside your head" that you use when trying to learn new information.

Standing in the lobby of the registrar's office, while repeating your new password over and over again, you might become distracted by two questions:

1. What is the capacity of working memory? That is, how much information can working memory hold at any one time? Could you keep an eight-digit password in your head? What if the password had sixteen digits?

2. How long does information stay in working memory?

If you kept repeating the password over and over, it could stay in your working memory forever, or at least until you went to sleep. But how long would the password remain in memory if you stopped repeating it? This activity is designed to provide an answer to that question.

TIPS

- Do not write the letter strings down! The goal is not to see how many letter strings you can get correct. The goal is to see how long unrehearsed information remains in working memory.

- If you are in a private location, do the subtraction task out loud. This will make it harder for you to rehearse the letters covertly during the subtraction task. On a similar note, do the subtraction task as quickly as possible. Again, this will make it much harder for you to cheat by rehearsing the letters while doing the subtraction.

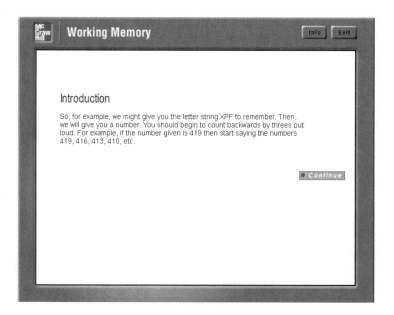

Working Memory
Info Exit

Introduction

So, for example, we might give you the letter string XPF to remember. Then, we will give you a number. You should begin to count backwards by threes out loud. For example, if the number given is 419 then start saying the numbers 419, 416, 413, 410, etc.

Continue

REFLECTION QUESTIONS

1. You are running a seminar on working memory to help people remember their grocery lists. What is one tip you can tell your class that will *increase* their chances of remembering their grocery items? What is one thing you can tell your class that they should *not* do when trying to remember their grocery lists?

2. You are at a cocktail party and are meeting a lot of new people. You really want to remember the names of all the people you meet. Based on what you know about working memory, why might this be a difficult task? What are some of the problems you might encounter using the methods that you learned in this exercise?

MULTIPLE-CHOICE ITEMS

1. Which of the following best describes working memory?
   a. a place where brief sensory representations are stored for less than one second
   b. a vast storage place where memories can be stored for a very long time
   c. an active workplace where information is retrieved, manipulated, and held through rehearsal
   d. a place where memories about one's occupation or educational pursuits are held

2. The working-memory demonstration showed that
   a. after eighteen seconds, about half of the unrehearsed items had faded from working memory.
   b. after eighteen seconds, most of the unrehearsed items had faded from working memory.
   c. after six seconds, all of the unrehearsed items had faded from working memory.
   d. after six seconds, none of the unrehearsed items had faded from working memory.

3. One conclusion you can make based on the working-memory demonstration is that
   a. when trying to recall a letter string, the time delay between seeing that item and remembering it does not matter if you are not allowed to rehearse the item.
   b. the longer the delay between study and recall, the greater the likelihood of accurately recalling a letter string.
   c. unless a letter string represents something real, it is impossible to remember it regardless of the time delay between learning and recall.
   d. without rehearsal, it is easier to remember a letter string when time delays between learning and recall are shorter.

4. John is very hungry and decides to call in a pizza order. He looks up the phone number but realizes that his phone is across the room. The best way for John to remember the phone number by the time he reaches his phone is for him to
   a. repeat the phone number over and over as he walks to his phone.
   b. try to empty his mind of any thoughts as he walks to his phone.
   c. try to recall similar phone numbers he has dialed in the past as he walks to his phone.
   d. focus on the first three digits of the phone number, as the rest will not have faded from working memory.

5. One way researchers test the duration of working memory is to
   a. have a person view a very brief flash of a matrix of items and immediately recall as many items as they can remember.
   b. have a person sleep between learning the information and performing a memory test on that information.
   c. have a person listen to two streams of information but pay attention to only one stream of information.
   d. have a person perform a distraction task to prevent rehearsal of the to-be-remembered items for varying lengths of time.

7.3 Working Memory: Putting Memory to Work

Have you ever had a server in a restaurant who remembered the orders of a large number of people perfectly without writing anything down? How did that person hold all of that information in his or her head if the capacity of short-term memory is "the magical number 7 ± 2"? It turns out that people in the restaurant business employ a variety of mental strategies to help them remember strings of orders. Many of these principles are well known by psychologists. This activity will give you some experience working in a virtual restaurant. First, you will try to remember a series of orders by using your wits. Then you will receive some training in using the techniques that are commonly employed informally in restaurants and more formally in cognitive psychology experiments to help you remember all the orders for your tables. The activity will also explain the structure of memory to help you better understand *why* these techniques are effective. This is very important because, as you saw at the beginning of this course, the goal of psychological research is not to understand what people do but rather why they do what they do.

- Choose a different set of tables, and run through the simulation a second time. Did you do better or worse on the novel set of tables? Challenge one of your friends to remember the items from the same set of tables. Did your newly acquired skills enable you to remember more items than your friend could?

- Expertise is another important factor in training your memory. Although servers are very good at remembering long strings of meal orders, they may be no better than average at remembering a series of directions for driving through a city. Taxi drivers, on the other hand, need to be very good at remembering driveable routes in their own city but need be no better than average at remembering long strings of meal orders.

REFLECTION QUESTION

On your first day as a new employee for Fabulous Shoes, every other worker calls in sick. Consequently, you are the only person handling the customers. When the store opens, four customers approach you immediately and ask you to retrieve shoes for them. Steve, a little boy, needs size 1 snow boots. Hilda, a tall woman, needs size 9 silver dress shoes. Oscar, a skinny, short man, needs size 9 running shoes. Finally, Eloise, an older grandmother, needs size 9 slippers. Based on the principles of working memory and associated memory techniques, what are some strategies you can use to help you select the correct shoes for each customer?

1. The component of working memory that plans and controls its various subsystems is called the
   a. central executive.
   b. phonological loop.
   c. episodic buffer.
   d. visuospatial sketchpad.

2. When Rose meets a new person, she repeats the person's name over and over in her head in an attempt to remember that name at a later time. Which part of working memory is activated by this activity?
   a. central executive
   b. phonological loop
   c. episodic buffer
   d. visuospatial sketchpad

3. Paul is driving to his friend Peter's house for the first time. Paul has a map, but because he is on a busy highway, he can glance at the map only every few minutes. Between these glances, Paul keeps a picture of the map in his head by using the _____ component of working memory.
   a. central executive
   b. phonological loop
   c. episodic buffer
   d. visuospatial sketchpad

4. Sylvie asks her brother Sam if she can borrow his car. Sam says she can if she will first go to the car and retrieve his Rihanna CD from his giant CD collection. So that she won't forget which CD Sam wants, Sylvie imagines a picture of Rihanna in her head while humming the song "Umbrella" as she walks to the car. Sylvie is relying on which component(s) of working memory to help her out?
   a. phonological loop
   b. visuospatial sketchpad
   c. Both a and b
   d. Neither a nor b

5. Desmond must enter a long string of numbers (1 4 9 2 1 6 2 0 1 7 7 6) into an old computer every two hours or the computer will mysteriously shut down. Desmond finds that combining the numbers into three meaningful years (1492, 1620, 1776) makes it easier for him to remember the string. Desmond is relying on which memory aid to help him recall the numbers?
   a. acronyms
   b. chunking
   c. consolidation
   d. visual imagery

7.4 Long-Term Memory

Think back on an important event from your life (e.g., high school graduation, passing your driver's test, an argument with a parent or significant other). Chances are, you can see these events clearly in your mind. You can relive them, too, mentally watching them replay in your head over and over again. This experience leads many people to believe that memories are like computer files or bits of recorded television shows. When we want to reexperience a past event—that is, remember it—we simply hit the play button on our mental-event recorders. Cognitive psychologists do not believe that memory works this way. Instead, they believe that knowledge of the past consists of many distinct elements and that our experience of remembering a particular event occurs when these distinct elements are all brought "online" at the same time. The first video you watch will try to make this line of reasoning clear. Errors or gaps in memory occur when the different pieces do not fit together neatly or when one or more pieces cannot be retrieved. This is not to say that memory is always error-prone. Under certain circumstances, memory can be remarkably clear and precise. The second video interviews some "memory athletes," people who have trained their minds to memorize the order of a shuffled deck of cards, for instance, in a matter of minutes.

TIPS

- The first video briefly mentions that past knowledge influences our memory of an object or event. One interesting way to see this is to visit your old elementary school and note how much smaller your classroom and desks are than you remember them.

- What makes Tatiana's memory so good? According to her, it's not that she is uniquely gifted. Instead, she has a system for associating items with one another. Think about how her strategy fits with the theories proposed by the psychologists in the first video.

REFLECTION QUESTION

Mnemonic strategies can be used for a variety of situations, including remembering grocery lists or the names of new people you meet. For example, imagery can be used to help remember pairs of words (e.g., brick-hand). You create an image for each word and then connect the two images through visualization (e.g., a hand lifting a brick). Consider the following five pairs of words: (1) table-rabbit; (2) box-tulip; (3) telephone-jackhammer; (4) candle-key; (5) finger-apple. Imagine both words in each word pair, and connect them to form a visual image. Wait for five minutes and try to recall the pairs (don't peek!). How did you do? Did you find this technique useful?

MULTIPLE-CHOICE ITEMS

1. According to research on memory,
   a. most people can improve their memory dramatically using various memory techniques.
   b. only a small percentage of people can improve their memory dramatically using various memory techniques.
   c. about 5 percent of the population has a photographic memory.
   d. memory ability is genetically determined and cannot be improved with practice.

2. Tatiana, the woman in the video, was able to memorize the order of cards in a standard deck by
   a. picturing each card in her head for a few seconds.
   b. assigning each card a word based on a coding system and telling a story with the cards.
   c. visualizing each card at a specific location in her apartment.
   d. making a rhyme for each card as it was presented.

3. One good memory technique, which was demonstrated by the man in the classroom who memorized the last digit of every student's Social Security number, is that of
   a. imagining each number as sitting on top of the appropriate student's head.
   b. mentally reordering the numbers in sequential order.
   c. rehearsing the string of numbers over and over in one's head.
   d. grouping the numbers and assigning meaning to each sequence.

4. Research investigating champion chess players' memory for the location of chess pieces on a board demonstrated that
   a. expertise in chess had no effect on one's ability to remember the layout of a chess board.
   b. the champions were unable to remember the placement of more than two or three pieces for any of the boards.
   c. memory for a board from an actual chess game was far superior to memory for a board with randomly placed chess pieces.
   d. memory for a board from an actual chess game was equal to memory for a board with randomly placed chess pieces.

5. MRI (brain-imaging) studies found that greater activity was apparent in which lobe(s) when participants were focused on the meaning of words they were to remember later?
   a. frontal lobe only
   b. temporal lobe only
   c. frontal lobe and temporal lobe
   d. frontal lobe, temporal lobe, and parietal lobe

7.5 Levels of Processing: Transferring Information from Short-Term Memory to Long-Term Memory

We have learned that rehearsing information tends to help it stick in memory better. Some psychologists would say that rehearsal enables us to transfer information from "short-term memory" into "long-term memory." There are many different methods to rehearse new information, with some rehearsal strategies being much more effective than others. This activity will illustrate *levels-of-processing theory.* Briefly, this theory argues that the more one thinks about the meaning of an item in short-term memory, the more likely it is to be transferred to long-term memory and the more likely it is to be remembered later. According to this theory, thinking about the meaning of an item is more likely to integrate the item with information already stored in long-term memory, thus locking it in place. This explains why it is easier to remember a computer password that has a meaning (a word, abbreviation, or acronym) than it is to remember one that is a random string of letters and numbers.

TIPS

- Do not respond too quickly to the questions about the words in the activity. Accuracy is important here because it ensures that you have thought about the relevant dimensions of each word.

- Another way to demonstrate levels of processing would be to repeat Activity 7.2 "Working Memory." This time, try to form meaningful associations among the three letters you are trying to remember. If you do this effectively, it is often possible to retain the letters even after eighteen seconds of counting backward.

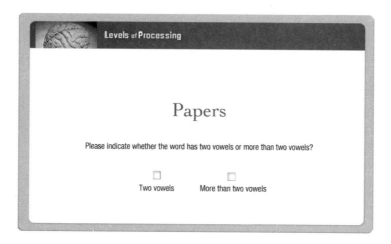

REFLECTION QUESTION

You are a teaching assistant for an introductory psychology class. The professor has put you in charge of leading a study session for the first exam. Luckily, you have just learned about levels of processing. Based on your knowledge of levels of processing, how will you instruct the students to study the test material? What are two examples of effective study tips? two examples of ineffective study tips?

MULTIPLE-CHOICE ITEMS

1. Levels of processing is defined as
   a. the degree to which new material is mentally analyzed.
   b. the number of neural centers that the information must pass through on its way to the brain.
   c. the variety of stimuli encountered in an episode.
   d. the distinction between auditory, tactile, and visual processing.

2. Which example represents the most shallow level of processing?
   a. determining the meaning of the word
   b. determining if a word is in all capital letters or not
   c. determining if a word properly completes a sentence or not
   d. determining if a word has a positive or a negative emotional connotation

3. According to levels-of-processing theory,
   a. the deeper you process information, the more likely you will remember it.
   b. shallow processing is best for long-term memory, while deep processing is best for short-term memory.
   c. when trying to memorize information, the time spent studying the information is more important than the way the information is processed.
   d. analyzing the superficial characteristics of the to-be-remembered information leads to better memory than analyzing the meaning of the to-be-remembered information.

4. Catie meets a boy named Hunter and really wants to remember his name so that she can impress him the next time she sees him. According to levels-of-processing theory, she should
   a. count the number of vowels and consonants in his name.
   b. repeat his name over and over as he walks away.
   c. visualize the actual letters of the word *Hunter*.
   d. focus on the meaning of *Hunter* and imagine a hunter in the woods.

5. _____ is to shallow processing as _____ is to deep processing
   a. Meaning; repetition
   b. Repetition; meaning
   c. Repetition; number
   d. Number; meaning

7.6 Eyewitness Fallibility: Witnessing a Crime

As you have no doubt experienced, memory is not perfect. We forget to meet a friend for dinner or write a paper due in a class. Usually the cost of these errors is minimal. Our friend will forgive us, and perhaps our professor will let us turn the paper in late. However, in legal settings the imperfection of memory can have dire consequences. Innocent people have often been convicted based on faulty eyewitness testimony and been freed only when DNA evidence proved that they were innocent. The first video that you are about to watch ("When Eyes Deceive") will provide a powerful demonstration of how poorly people perform when asked to identify the person who committed a crime that they witnessed. Research has shown that eyewitness errors can result from a number of sources, including subtle or covert suggestions, pressure from law-enforcement officials, biases on the part of the witness, and a lack of attention to detail because of the stress of being victimized. Fortunately, psychological science has provided some tools that law-enforcement officials can use to increase the probability that an eyewitness will be able to provide complete and accurate descriptions of a criminal. Some of these procedures are detailed in the second video ("False Memories").

TIPS

- As you watch the second video, think about how you might have applied the details of the cognitive interview to help identify the criminal presented in the first video.

- See how the powerful effect of suggestion by an authority figure is demonstrated in each of the videos. This is a very important influence on the accuracy of eyewitness testimony. How do you think this factor might be observed in investigations of real-world crimes?

  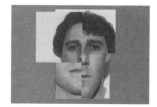

REFLECTION QUESTION

Many people place items in locations for safekeeping. Sadly, we often forget these locations when we need these items. Sometimes we lose items not because we hid them temporarily but because we forgot where we put them down. Think about the last time you were unable to find your keys or wallet or some other item. Do you think the principles of the cognitive interview would have helped you locate the item? In particular, what aspects of the procedure do you think would have been helpful?

MULTIPLE-CHOICE ITEMS

1. In using the "standard" interview technique, a police officer would
   a. interrupt the witness with frequent questions.
   b. help the witness remain calm and relaxed during the interview.
   c. ask the witness to assume the perspective of another participant in the event.
   d. instruct the witness to use reverse-order recall.

2. In using the "cognitive interview" technique, a police office would
   a. focus on the details of the crime first, while they were still fresh in the witness's memory.
   b. begin with the broad outlines of the crime and then follow up by asking the witness about specific details.
   c. re-ask the same questions multiple times to ensure that the subject gave the same response each time.
   d. use leading questions to guide the witness through the sequence of events in a logical order.

3. Compared to standard interview techniques, the cognitive interview
   a. can be used effectively for nonviolent crimes but not for violent ones.
   b. can be used effectively for violent crimes but not for nonviolent ones.
   c. is more effective at eliciting accurate information.
   d. is not more effective at eliciting accurate information but allows the police to gather information more quickly.

4. Leading questions
   a. are designed to lead the witness through the sequence of events in a logical order.
   b. are designed to mislead the witness in order to assess how much confidence to place in her or his memory.
   c. often help the witness find new information.
   d. often lead the witness to "remember" inaccurate information.

5. The cognitive interview relies heavily on
   a. auditory sensory memory.
   b. visual sensory memory.
   c. both auditory and visual sensory memory.
   d. cognitive memory rather than sensory memory of any kind.

7.7 Eyewitness Fallibility: Focusing Attention

People are frequently convicted of crimes they did not commit. Often these cases turn on eyewitness testimony. A victim or someone at the scene of the crime confidently—but incorrectly—identifies the defendant. You may wonder how it is possible that someone could be wrong about something so important. There are many explanations for how memory can go tragically awry. This activity will highlight one of them: lack of attention. Sometimes, people miss the details of an event because they were not paying close, careful attention at the time the event took place. This activity will measure your ability to concentrate in a very distracting environment to see how lapses of attention can cause memory failures.

T I P S

- Watch the players in the white shirts carefully. The video is somewhat grainy (on purpose) to make the viewing conditions more challenging.

- Make sure that you watch the video by yourself. Do not have anyone looking over your shoulder, as this person may distract you.

- Think about why our memory system might have evolved to keep information out.

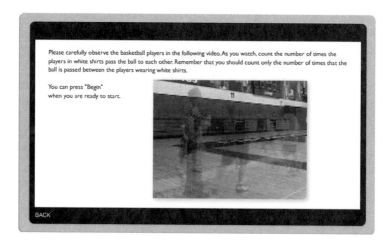

Please carefully observe the basketball players in the following video. As you watch, count the number of times the players in white shirts pass the ball to each other. Remember that you should count only the number of times that the ball is passed between the players wearing white shirts.

You can press "Begin" when you are ready to start.

BACK

REFLECTION QUESTION

You have just been hired as chief security officer for a large office building. The building owners want to buy you a fancy video surveillance system where you can sit in a room and watch what is going on in various locations of the building. They want you to design the best system (e.g., one screen that alternates recordings of various locations, multiple screens that you can view at once) for accurate surveillance. Based on what you know about eyewitness fallibility and sensory memory, what system would you design and why?

MULTIPLE-CHOICE ITEMS

1. For information to enter into long-term memory, it must first
   a. pass first through sensory memory and then short-term memory.
   b. pass through only sensory memory
   c. pass first through short-term memory and then sensory memory.
   d. pass through only short-term memory.

2. Sensory memory is most like
   a. a photograph that is ruined almost immediately after it is taken.
   b. a story you retell several times.
   c. a dream you had in the distant past but still remember well.
   d. a vault that stores all of your life experiences.

3. Information from sensory memory will enter into short-term memory only
   a. after a delay of ten to fifteen seconds.
   b. if it is actually attended to while in sensory memory.
   c. when a person is awake.
   d. if it first filters through long-term memory.

4. Jill is shopping at a convenience store when a man runs in and points a gun at the clerk. The clerk gives the man money, and the man leaves. When Jill is questioned about the event, she clearly remembers the gun but has no idea what color shirt the perpetrator was wearing. According to the exercise, this is most likely because

   a. the man's shirt color was never represented in Jill's sensory memory.

   b. the man's shirt color entered Jill's long-term memory but is currently repressed.

   c. Jill was focused on the gun and, consequently, the man's shirt color never made it from her sensory memory to her short-term memory.

   d. Jill could not register details like shirt color in sensory memory because of the speed at which the event occurred.

5. According to research on eyewitness fallibility,

   a. people often forget some details of an event because they are focused on other aspects of the event.

   b. two people might remember very different components of a video, depending on what they are paying attention to while watching the video.

   c. although our sensory memory contains an exact copy of what we witness, only some of that information enters into short-term memory.

   d. All of the above.

7.8 Alzheimer's Disease

Alzheimer's disease is a progressive, debilitating mental disorder. Although its primary symptoms relate to memory, the loss of memory influences other aspects of personality, including temperament. Those who suffer from Alzheimer's disease often become irritable or depressed, presumably due to the frustration of living with the disease.

Alzheimer's disease is one example of a broader class of cognitive disorders called *dementia*. There are a variety of causes of dementia. Alzheimer's dementia results from a particular kind of damage to neurons in the brain. However, the memory loss associated with dementia can also result from oxygen deprivation, lifelong alcohol abuse, and even a long-standing, severe vitamin deficiency. Thus, it is essential that a person suffering from dementia receive proper medical attention.

TIPS

- It is normal for some memory loss to occur as one ages. As you watch the video of Helen, think about how her behavior differs from that of a healthy older adult that you know. Look beyond the memory deficits to other aspects of her personality, like how quiet and subdued Helen is.

- Keep in mind that Helen is at a moderate stage of dementia. Although she has difficulty recalling information from the recent past, she understands her daughter's question and is able to respond appropriately. As the disease progresses, these kinds of behavior are lost, in addition to the ability to remember personal details of one's life.

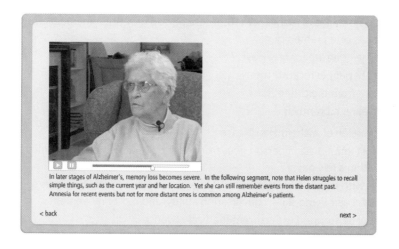

In later stages of Alzheimer's, memory loss becomes severe. In the following segment, note that Helen struggles to recall simple things, such as the current year and her location. Yet she can still remember events from the distant past. Amnesia for recent events but not for more distant ones is common among Alzheimer's patients.

< back   next >

REFLECTION QUESTION

You may know a person or a family that has dealt with Alzheimer's disease or a similar form of dementia. What were the first signs of the disease? How did the disease progress? How has it affected the person's family? (If you don't know of a person or a family afflicted by the disease, describe the typical progression and effects of the disease.)

MULTIPLE-CHOICE ITEMS

1. Alzheimer's disease is caused by
   a. an organic brain disorder that kills brain cells.
   b. several small strokes that damage the brain.
   c. a severe lack of oxygen to the brain for several minutes.
   d. a blood clot that erupts in the brain.

2. Alzheimer's disease affects _____ percent of 75- to 84-year-old adults in the United States.
   a. 10
   b. 20
   c. 30
   d. 40

3. Which of the following is (are) symptomatic of Alzheimer's disease?
   a. memory loss
   b. disorientation
   c. impaired motor activities
   d. All of the above

4. In the middle stages of Alzheimer's disease, a person may not remember where she or he is but can often remember
   a. what she or he ate for breakfast.
   b. names of people recently met.
   c. an event from the distant past.
   d. what year it currently is.

5. The progression of Alzheimer's disease
   a. is almost immediate: a person goes from near-perfect memory to complete memory loss within a few days.
   b. begins with simple forgetfulness and over the course of years becomes so severe that it affects basic living skills, conversation ability, and motor movement.
   c. can now be stopped with current medical advances.
   d. is often reversed with a few simple memory-training sessions.

CHAPTER EIGHT

Language, Cognition, and Intelligence

8.1 Thinking and Reasoning: Centenarians

Often, the images that come to mind when we think of aging are unpleasant. We think of physical decline, loss of independence, and especially cognitive decline. Most people associate aging with a loss of memory or mental sharpness. As you will see in this video, the decline in memory is not a foregone conclusion. Some people remain cognitively fit for as long as they remain physically fit—and sometimes longer. According to this video, one of the things that seems to distinguish people who remain cognitively fit into old age is their lifelong love of learning. They continue to engage in mentally taxing events long after their formal schooling ends. Psychologists sometimes refer to this explanation for spared cognitive functioning in old age as "use it or lose it." Understanding what factors may help promote cognitive abilities in old age is important as medical science and improved health care in general continue to expand life expectancies.

TIPS

- Think about some adults in your own life who may or may not have remained cognitively healthy into old age. Do they fit the pattern you would expect from the use-it-or-lose-it theory? As you watch the video, think about why cognitive "exercise" might preserve mental functioning.

- Recent work by Timothy Salthouse has called the use-it-or-lose-it theory into question, so it is currently unclear whether mental activity really does preserve cognitive functioning. More generally, it is important to remember that scientific ideas are constantly undergoing revision and reevaluation.

REFLECTION QUESTION

Some recent research has suggested that college professors tend to retain their cognitive abilities better in old age than do people in other professions. How might you explain this finding by using the theories presented in this video?

MULTIPLE-CHOICE ITEMS

1. Mental exercise
   a. improves emotional health but has negative effects on cognitive health.
   b. improves cognitive health but has negative effects on emotional health.
   c. improves cognitive health but has neutral effects on physical health.
   d. has no known effect on cognitive, emotional, or physical health.

2. Learning new skills in old age can help memory by fostering
   a. creativity.
   b. curiosity.
   c. the growth of new neurons.
   d. the growth of new connections between existing neurons.

3. Harry's ability to recall a sequence of digits was
   a. much worse than you would expect from someone his age.
   b. much better than you would expect of someone his age but not very good for a younger adult.
   c. much better than you would expect even from someone much younger than Harry.
   d. None of the above.

4. Harry attributes his longevity to
   a. regular, moderate, physical exercise.
   b. a commitment to a healthful diet.
   c. his love of music, literature, and art.
   d. the love and support of family and friends.

5. The benefits of mental exercise are seen most strongly in people
   a. with low IQ scores.
   b. with high IQ scores.
   c. who start learning new things in old age.
   d. who show a lifelong love of learning new things.

8.2 Heuristics

Speedy Sara and Slow-and-Steady Zak both need the same book from the library to write a paper for their Asian American–studies class. Zak writes the title of the book on a piece of paper, then heads to the library. He picks up the first book he finds and reads the title to see if it matches the title written on his sheet of paper. Slowly and steadily, he makes his way from floor to floor, checking every book in the building until he finds the one he is looking for. Sara writes the call number of the book on a piece of paper, uses the library map to find the appropriate shelf in the library, and begins her search there.

Clearly, Speedy Sara has adopted the better strategy. She will find the book first unless, by sheer luck, Zak begins his search in the exact right location. However, what would happen if the book were accidentally shelved in the wrong location? In this case, Zak would eventually find the book, but Sara probably would not.

Our cognitive system often faces problems when two solutions are available: one that is very time consuming but will invariably lead to success (like Zak's) and another that is faster, easier, and works well most of the time (like Sara's). Psychologists refer to these kinds of simple but potentially error-prone solutions as *heuristics*. Because we are bombarded by information, our cognitive systems frequently employ heuristics to help us make decisions quickly and efficiently. Most of the time, we are unaware of these heuristics, because they work pretty well. The current activity was designed to demonstrate a situation in which a commonly used heuristic leads to a decision-making error.

TIPS

- Don't waste time or energy trying to remember the names on the list. The activity instructions were not designed to mislead you. This really is not a memory test.

- The fact that the names on the lists are presented in two different colors is also not relevant to the point of the activity. Just follow the instructions, and think about each of the names as it appears on the screen.

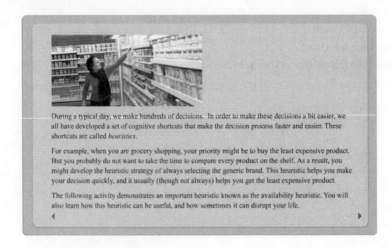

During a typical day, we make hundreds of decisions. In order to make these decisions a bit easier, we all have developed a set of cognitive shortcuts that make the decision process faster and easier. These shortcuts are called *heuristics*.

For example, when you are grocery shopping, your priority might be to buy the least expensive product. But you probably do not want to take the time to compare every product on the shelf. As a result, you might develop the heuristic strategy of always selecting the generic brand. This heuristic helps you make your decision quickly, and it usually (though not always) helps you get the least expensive product.

The following activity demonstrates an important heuristic known as the availability heuristic. You will also learn how this heuristic can be useful, and how sometimes it can disrupt your life.

REFLECTION QUESTIONS

1. Do you think more people die from shark attacks or from falling airplane parts? You might be surprised to learn that you are thirty times more likely to die from a falling airplane part than from a shark attack. Using what you have learned about the availability heuristic, why do you think this is so?

2. You are the campaign manager for Ima Winner, who is running for mayor in your hometown. Using the availability heuristic, what are two things you can do to increase Ima's chances of winning the election?

MULTIPLE-CHOICE ITEMS

1. A cognitive shortcut that speeds decision making is called a(n)
   a. mnemonic.   b. schema.   c. heuristic.   d. assimilation.

2. The availability heuristic suggests that
   a. we categorize information based on how representative it is of a stereotype.
   b. we judge the probability of an event on the size of the competing sample.
   c. we base the frequencies of events on the ease to which information regarding that event comes to mind.
   d. we use others' responses to questions if they are available to us.

3. People use heuristics because
   a. they save us time.   c. they often lead to correct responses.
   b. they save us cognitive energy.   d. All of the above

4. Ellen's best friend won the lottery with the numbers 4, 8, 15, 16, 23, 42. Now, Ellen buys a lottery ticket every day choosing these same numbers because she is convinced that she too will win. What error in judgment is Ellen making?
   a. The likelihood of the same numbers winning again is significantly less than other number combinations.
   b. Rare but highly memorable events that easily come to mind increase our beliefs they will happen again—even when they don't.
   c. Ellen is mistakenly relying on the consistency heuristic and should pick different numbers each day.
   d. Ellen is basing her decision on too large a sample size.

5. Which of the following is an example of the availability heuristic?
   a. Bill's brother is injured in the bathtub, so Bill will only take showers, because he is afraid that bathtubs are unnecessarily dangerous.
   b. John meets a person named Summer who has blond hair and a tan. Summer is a vegetarian and likes to surf. John assumes Summer is from California.
   c. Gil puts two red balls and two blue balls in a bag. Blindfolded, he pulls out the first ball and it is red. Gil assumes the next ball he will pull out of the bag will be blue.
   d. Matt is 5 feet 7 inches tall and his wife, Tammy, is 5 feet 3 inches tall. Matt is convinced that their son Jake will be at least 5 feet 10 inches tall.

8.3 Gardner's Theory of Multiple Intelligences

You may be surprised to learn that formal intelligence tests are a relatively recent development. The first wave of modern intelligence tests was developed in the late nineteenth century. Many theorists have been critical of these and more recent intelligence tests because they equate intelligence with academic knowledge or book smarts. This should not be surprising, however, given that the people who developed these tests were academics who spent much of their lives acquiring book smarts. In recent years, there have been many attempts to broaden the definition of intelligence, but one question that has remained is whether intelligence is a single trait or whether there are different kinds of intelligence. This activity will give you an opportunity to learn about one way of splitting intelligence into multiple components: Howard Gardner's theory of multiple intelligences.

TIP

- Skip over the descriptions of the different kinds of intelligence, and complete the quiz first. Then go back and read the descriptions. This way your responses will reflect your actual view of yourself, rather than the way you want to perceive yourself.

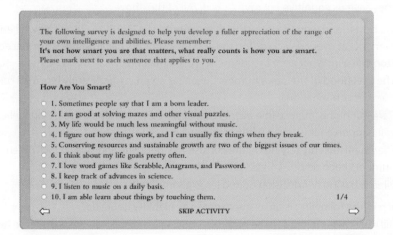

The following survey is designed to help you develop a fuller appreciation of the range of your own intelligence and abilities. Please remember:
It's not how smart you are that matters, what really counts is how you are smart.
Please mark next to each sentence that applies to you.

How Are You Smart?

1. Sometimes people say that I am a born leader.
2. I am good at solving mazes and other visual puzzles.
3. My life would be much less meaningful without music.
4. I figure out how things work, and I can usually fix things when they break.
5. Conserving resources and sustainable growth are two of the biggest issues of our times.
6. I think about my life goals pretty often.
7. I love word games like Scrabble, Anagrams, and Password.
8. I keep track of advances in science.
9. I listen to music on a daily basis.
10. I am able learn about things by touching them.

1/4

◁   SKIP ACTIVITY   ▷

REFLECTION QUESTION

You just completed a questionnaire that highlighted your relative interests and abilities according to Gardner's theory of multiple intelligences. Do you think that your personal summary accurately reflects your strengths and weaknesses? Do you wish you were stronger in certain areas? According to Gardner, what are some occupations that you would be well suited for?

MULTIPLE-CHOICE ITEMS

1. A single general ability that influences all areas of intellectual functioning is called the
   a. central domain.
   b. multimodal approach.
   c. G-factor.
   d. primary factor.

2. According to Gardner,
   a. a single general ability underlies all of our abilities to adapt to our environment.
   b. intelligence is a complex set of abilities made up of several distinct but related domains.
   c. intelligence cannot be measured by paper-and-pencil tests.
   d. intelligence cannot be improved with experience.

3. Jim loves the outdoors. He is interested in different types of plants and flowers and also likes digging for fossils and old artifacts. Jim is most likely strong in which type of intelligence?
   a. linguistic
   b. kinesthetic
   c. naturalist
   d. logical

4. Terry often gets lost when driving places. It seems he just can't understand maps and often confuses north with south. Terry is probably weak in which type of intelligence?
   a. linguistic
   b. kinesthetic
   c. logical
   d. spatial

5. Anthea is people smart. She is good at reading the feelings and emotions of others and can predict other people's intentions. According to Gardner, for which occupation is Anthea well suited?
   a. social worker
   b. critic
   c. tour guide
   d. author

8.4 IQ Tests: Are They Accurate Measures of Intelligence?

Standardized tests have become what Dr. Stephen Ceci calls gatekeepers. That is, they determine what kinds of educational and economic opportunities a person will have. College-bound students take the SAT or ACT to determine what kind of college they will be able to attend—or whether they will be able to attend college at all. Many states now employ regular testing through elementary and secondary schools to measure whether students are making adequate educational progress. Some of these tests are appropriately labeled "high-stakes tests" because students who fail to achieve a certain score on them are not able to graduate. Given the importance of these tests, one would hope that we could have confidence in how well they measure intelligence. According to Dr. Ceci, however, we should not have much confidence in these measures. In these videos, Dr. Ceci describes some of the problems associated with an overreliance on standardized tests as measures of intelligence, the reasons why these tests are relied on so heavily, and some alternative ways that we might measure human intelligence.

T I P

- Intelligence-testing theorists generally fall into two categories. Some believe that intelligence is a single thing that can be applied to many different settings. Others see intelligence as consisting of many different skills, so that a person can have lots of intelligence in one area but relatively little in another. As you listen to Dr. Ceci talk, think about whether he seems to endorse the single- or multiple-ability view of intelligence.

Steve Ceci, Ph.D.
Cornell University

REFLECTION QUESTION

When Dr. Ceci asserts that the best predictor of a child's IQ is the size of the parents' bank account, he is *not* saying that rich people are smarter than poor people. What point is he trying to make?

MULTIPLE-CHOICE ITEMS

1. The fact that many Category 4 soldiers completed their basic training with little or no difficulty suggests that
   a. military achievement tests are culturally biased.
   b. the military would be better served if it adopted the SAT instead of its current intelligence test.
   c. whatever the military tests measured was not predictive of performance in a military setting.
   d. military training requires little or no intelligence.

2. Dr. Ceci states that achievement tests do "reflect some native abilities, but a very small spectrum and very imperfectly." Based on this quote, it is likely that he views intelligence as
   a. a single mental ability that underlies performance in a variety of settings.
   b. a large number of different mental abilities that may be present in different quantities within an individual person.
   c. something that is easily measured by standardized tests.
   d. something that cannot be evaluated with any level of precision no matter how one tests an individual.

3. According to Dr. Ceci, college-admissions committees have trouble evaluating applicants because there is a great deal of variability in
   a. letters of recommendation.
   b. personal experiences.
   c. the level of intellectual challenge across courses at different high schools.
   d. the kinds of skills measured by achievement tests.

4. Dr. Ceci suggests that college-admissions committees should evaluate applicants by
   a. developing new achievement tests based on more rigorous versions of questions that currently are included in the SAT.
   b. having students complete personality tests in addition to the standard achievement tests.
   c. meeting all applicants in person so that experienced interviewers can assess how well high school grades and SAT scores reflect each applicant's true abilities.
   d. directly measuring the applicant's ability to perform the kinds of tasks they will be asked to perform in college.

5. Parents who gain more education tend to have kids who score better on IQ tests because
   a. more highly educated parents tend to provide more intellectually stimulating environments to their children.
   b. education improves the genes that are passed on to the children.
   c. education improves economic standing, which enables parents to enroll their children in IQ-building preschool programs.
   d. None of the above

8.5 Group Differences in IQ

A great deal of controversy surrounds the performance of different ethnic groups on standardized tests of intelligence and achievement. No one debates that the average performance of Caucasian students is higher than the average performance of African American and Latino students. The controversy has to do with the *causes* of these ethnic differences. Some theorists have looked to nature as an explanation, claiming that there are inherent genetic differences between racial groups. Other theorists tend to explain group differences in terms of environmental factors, including socioeconomic status, access to educational resources, and parental education. Much of the current debate was stimulated by *The Bell Curve,* a book by Edward Herrnstein and Charles Murray. This book took a very strong stand arguing against environmental factors, and the ensuing controversy led the APA to commission a task force to study the issue. The report in this activity provides an excellent review of the scientific literature on intelligence.

TIPS

- The task force's article is quite long. It covers a lot of ground, including basic theories of intelligence. Sections 3 ("The Genes and Intelligence"), 4 ("Environmental Effects on Intelligence,"), and 5 ("Group Differences") are the most relevant to the current issue. Given that this is an introductory psychology course rather than a course on intelligence or individual differences, you may start with Section 6 ("Summary and Conclusions"), then move to the earlier sections to fill in the details regarding the research that led to the conclusions drawn at the end of the paper.

- The task force's article critiques some of the debate as being a function of political views rather than scientific evidence. Bear in mind that you should not accept or reject the task force's claims simply because they match or do not match your political views. As a scientist, you should seek to find works that support the arguments made in *The Bell Curve* and compare the evidence they present with the evidence presented by the task force.

Intelligence: Knowns and Unknowns

Ulric Neisser (Chair)	*Emory University*
Gwyneth Boodoo	*Educational Testing Service, Princeton, New Jersey*
Thomas J. Bouchard, Jr.	*University of Minnesota, Minneapolis*
A. Wade **Boykin**	*Howard University*
Nathan Brody	*Wesleyan University*
Stephen J. Ceci	*Cornell University*
Diane F. Halpern	*California State University, San Bernardino*
John C. Loehlin	*University of Texas, Austin*
Robert Perloff	*University of Pittsburgh*
Robert J. Sternberg	*Yale University*
Susana Urbina	*University of North Florida*

In the fall of 1994, the publication of Herrnstein and ***Murray's*** *book The Bell Curve sparked a new round of debate about the meaning of intelligence test scores and the nature of intelligence. The debate was characterized by strong assertions as well as by strong feelings. Unfortunately, those assertions often revealed serious misunderstandings of what has (and has not) been demonstrated by* **scientific** *research in this* **field.** *Although a great deal is now known, the issues remain complex and in many cases still unresolved. Another unfortunate aspect of the debate was that many participants made little* ***effort*** *to distinguish scientific issues from political ones.* **Research** *findings were often assessed not so much*

1. Concepts of Intelligence

Individuals differ from one another in their ability to understand complex ideas, to adapt effectively to the environment, to learn from experience, to engage in various forms of reasoning, to overcome obstacles by taking thought. Although these individual differences can be substantial, they are never entirely consistent: A given person's intellectual performance will vary on different occasions, in different domains, as judged by different criteria. Concepts of "intelligence" are attempts to clarify and organize this complex set of phenomena. Although considerable clarity has been achieved in some areas, no such conceptualization has yet answered all the important

REFLECTION QUESTION

Whether or not genetic factors determine group differences in IQ is a very important question with significant scientific, political, social, and educational implications. Imagine that a scientific breakthrough allowed us to determine whether genes played little or no role in observed group differences in IQ test performance. What political, social, and/or educational changes would (or should) take place in light of such a finding?

MULTIPLE-CHOICE ITEMS

1. IQ tests are correlated with
   a. academic performance but not occupational status.
   b. occupational status but not academic performance.
   c. neither academic performance nor occupational status.
   d. both academic performance and occupational status.

2. According to the APA task force's article,
   a. preschool programs like Head Start have long-lasting effects on IQ.
   b. preschool programs have no effect on IQ scores, even while the student is attending the program.
   c. formal schooling affects IQ primarily by helping develop new intellectual skills.
   d. formal schooling affects IQ primarily by imparting additional knowledge.

3. The Flynn effects refers to the fact that IQ test scores have
   a. increased a large amount over the last fifty years.
   b. increased a small but significant amount over the last fifty years.
   c. decreased a small but significant amount over the last fifty years.
   d. decreased a large amount over the last fifty years.

4. Regarding the Black/White IQ test score difference, the APA task force suggests that
   a. there is conclusive evidence that genes explain the difference.
   b. there is conclusive evidence that cultural factors explain the difference.
   c. there are many plausible explanations for this difference, but it is difficult to confirm or eliminate most of them.
   d. the difference has not been demonstrated reliably.

5. Although standardized tests do measure some forms of intelligence, they generally fail to measure
   a. creativity.
   b. wisdom.
   c. interpersonal (social) ability.
   d. All of the above

8.6 Mental Retardation: Down Syndrome

Down syndrome is a genetic condition. Compared to the general population, people with Down syndrome are at increased risk for certain health problems such as congenital heart defects, digestive problems, and childhood leukemia. Despite these risks and because advances in medicine have rendered most of these health problems treatable, people with Down syndrome lead productive and fulfilling lives. Effective therapies continue to be developed that help to increase physical and cognitive skills. In growing numbers, children with Down syndrome and other cognitive and physical disabilities are included in general education classrooms, where they are learning with their non-disabled peers. The link below provides information about Down syndrome from the National Down Syndrome Society.

http://www.ndss.org/

REFLECTION QUESTION

The lives of people with intellectual disabilities have change dramatically over the past fifty or so years. Once the institutionalization of people with Down syndrome was common; now, more teens and adults with Down syndrome are graduating each year from high school, going to college, finding employment, and living independently. What kinds of changes do you think might be in store for the next generation of mentally handicapped people? What kinds of new educational, occupational, or social opportunities might become available? What will usher in these changes: new technologies, new social values, new treatments?

MULTIPLE-CHOICE ITEMS

1. Down syndrome is caused by
   a. missing genetic material occurring on one chromosome.
   b. extra genetic material occurring on one chromosome.
   c. missing genetic material occurring on multiple chromosomes.
   d. extra genetic material occurring on multiple chromosomes.

2. Which of the following physical characteristics is associated with Down syndrome?
   a. an excessive ability to extend the joints
   b. small skin folds on the inner corners of the eyes
   c. a single deep crease across the center of the palm
   d. All of the above

3. Down syndrome is
   a. caused by environmental factors.
   b. more common as the age of the mother increases.
   c. more common in women who smoke.
   d. more common in women who consume caffeine.

4. Although people have been aware of Down syndrome for centuries, the first description of an individual with the condition was published
   a. approximately 25 years ago.
   b. approximately 50 years ago.
   c. approximately 100 years ago.
   d. approximately 150 years ago.

8.7 Language Development

The sequence of first-language learning in infants and children appears remarkably similar across cultures. Infants coo, then gradually begin to make babbling sounds that reflect the speech sounds made by their parents or other caregivers. Eventually, individual words are learned and joined together until phrases and finally entire sentences are spoken. The complexity of utterances also increases slowly across the childhood years. Not only does the sequence of language acquisition seem to be universal, but the timing of these various milestones is also remarkably similar, even though cultures vary widely in terms of how much time and energy parents and caregivers devote to language training. In some cultures, parents spend a lot of time speaking directly with their infants and toddlers; in other cultures, parent–child conversations are more rare. One other aspect of language acquisition that appears to be universal is "motherese." Adults have a particular way of speaking to babies, using high pitches and exaggerated variations in pitch. The videos that you are about to see will show some examples of this motherese, as well as children at various ages demonstrating some of the linguistic skills they have acquired. (By the way, crying is often considered the first step in language acquisition!)

T I P

- It will not be apparent to you in the videos, but the old wives' tale about girls acquiring language earlier than boys appears to be true. Research shows, for example, that girls develop the ability to tell coherent stories much earlier than do boys and that this gender gap persists at least through adolescence and probably into adulthood.

REFLECTION QUESTION

In the storytelling segment, Rose mentions that after squirming on the princess, the worm got off and then "comed" to the tea party. Presumably, Rose's parents have always used the correct past tense: *came* rather than *comed*. If Rose has never heard the word *comed*, why does she use it? What does this simple error tell us about how children learn language?

MULTIPLE-CHOICE ITEMS

1. Motherese is a form of speech characterized by
    a. large swings in pitch.
    b. small swings in pitch.
    c. low volume, so as not to startle the baby.
    d. high volume, to maintain the baby's attention.

2. The video of 18-month-old Rose demonstrates that
    a. children acquire the basic rules of grammar before they learn much vocabulary.
    b. children acquire complex grammatical rules before they learn much vocabulary.
    c. children acquire a good deal of vocabulary before they understand much about grammar.
    d. None of the above

3. The video of Rose at 2 ½ years old demonstrates that she has learned
    a. how to formulate complete sentences.
    b. how to formulate questions.
    c. how to respond to questions.
    d. All of the above

Motivation and Emotion

9.1 The Need for Achievement

People often humans themselves from animals by arguing that people are motivated by more complex needs than are animals. Animals tend to be motivated by such basic needs as food, water, and shelter. In addition to these basic needs, people are motivated by secondary needs like the need for companionship or achievement. As the video in this activity describes, *achievement motivation* refers to the desire to attain goals or complete tasks. Psychologists believe that achievement motivation varies in people in the same way that physical characteristics vary. Just as some people grow to be taller than others, some feel the need to achieve more than others. Achievement motivation is not the same thing as ability. One can be strongly motivated to succeed even if one has little ability in a particular field. Think about how many young children are strongly motivated to become professional athletes. Many work very hard toward this goal, even though few have the physical ability to realize their dream.

Measuring achievement motivation can be tricky, because people may not be entirely honest about their feelings. A high school student might try to conceal his achievement motivation from his friends to avoid the possibility of being labeled a nerd or a geek or whatever term is currently in fashion. This is why psychologists use "projective" tests like the TAT (thematic apperception test) to measure achievement motivation. The TAT is a series of ambiguous pictures; no explicit references are made to achievement motivation when subjects view the pictures. This allows researchers to gain a better sense of what a person is thinking. Because the subjects do not know that the researchers are looking for signs of achievement motivation, they are less likely to conceal these feelings if they exist.

TIPS

- After watching the whole video, go back to the beginning and assess the relative achievement motivations of the four young people as they talk about their hopes for the future.
- Pay careful attention to the issue that Dr. Miller-Jones raises at the very end of the video regarding cultural differences in the definition of achievement.

1. Do you consider yourself a person high or low in need for achievement? Provide an example from your life (e.g., a grade you received, a game you played, money you earned) that supports your response.

2. Tim and Jim are playing a trivia game where the player can select the level of difficulty of the items he or she wishes to answer (easy, moderately difficult, very difficult). Tim has a low need for achievement, and Jim has a high need for achievement. What type of trivia items will Tim most likely select, and why? What type of items will Jim likely select, and why?

MULTIPLE-CHOICE ITEMS

1. Need for achievement is a(n)
   a. stable, learned characteristic in which a person obtains satisfaction by striving for and attaining a level of excellence.
   b. interest in establishing and maintaining relationships with other people.
   c. tendency to seek impact, control, or influence over others.
   d. desire to maintain a strong sense of order of one's life.

2. Carlotta has a high need for achievement. She is likely to
   a. enroll in an easy math course where she knows she will succeed without much effort.
   b. enroll in a mid-level math course where she will be challenged but also have a good opportunity for success if she works hard.
   c. enroll in a difficult math course that is so challenging that many of the brightest students will do poorly.
   d. stay away from math courses, because she is not interested in furthering her education.

3. People high in need for achievement
   a. desire to control others.
   b. desire to avoid failure.
   c. desire to achieve success.
   d. desire to be connected to others emotionally.

4. One way to measure need for achievement is to
   a. look for themes of control and influence in a person's reports of his or her dreams.
   b. measure how fast a person can complete a difficult maze after many repeated trials.
   c. show someone an ambiguous picture, have them write a story about it, and look for themes of achievement in the story.
   d. have someone study a list of words and then test his or her memory for the list both immediately and after one hour.

5. Bill has a low need for achievement. He has decided to work a crossword puzzle printed in the local newspaper. Bill has learned that the crossword puzzle is easiest on Monday but grows progressively harder throughout the week. Bill is most likely to
   a. attempt Monday's puzzle, because it is the easiest and he is not likely to have to struggle when completing it.
   b. attempt a puzzle midweek, because it won't be either too easy or too difficult.
   c. attempt all of the puzzles and work on each until it is completed.
   d. attempt a difficult Friday puzzle first, then attempt the easy Monday puzzle.

6. Which story reflects a high need for achievement?
   a. After many weeks of practice, Tessa wins a tennis tournament for players one level higher than the level at which she had previously competed.
   b. John has effectively convinced several of his peers to elect him president of his class.
   c. Sidney works very hard to maintain her friendships. For example, she often writes letters to people she has met during her travels overseas.
   d. Even though he is 17 years old, Marco signed up to compete in a ping-pong tournament for 14-year-olds because he is sure he won't lose any matches.

9.2 Emotion: Language of the Face

As Desmond Morris explains in this video, the human face is a remarkable communication tool. We are able to signal a wide range of emotional expressions to one another without saying a word. This ability is even more pronounced when dealing with people we know well. However, most of the facial expressions in the human repertoire are universal. That is, unlike hand gestures (see Desmond Morris's video "Emotion: Body Language," Activity 9.3), facial expressions for happiness, anger, sadness, surprise, and so forth are the same for people all over the world. Moreover, the facial expressions that we use to communicate aggression or submission are very similar to those used by primates, which suggests there may be an evolutionary explanation for the cultural universality of facial expressions.

- Paul Ekman is a psychologist who did much of the pioneering work on the universality of facial expressions. More about his work can be found at paulekman.com (but be warned that there is a strong commercial element to this site).

- For those whose sports interests do not reach beyond North American football, the group of men performing the Maori ritual is the New Zealand national rugby team (nicknamed the All Blacks). It is definitely worth searching the Internet for "All Blacks Haka" or "Rugby Haka."

- Two related activities are:
  - Desmond Morris's "Emotion: Body Language" (Activity 9.3), which talks about cultural differences in the use of hand gestures and body language.
  - "Detection of Deception" (Activity 9.4), which discusses the differences between true smiles and forced smiles; the video describes how these differences may be used to detect whether someone is or is not telling the truth.

REFLECTION QUESTION

Unlike body language (see Desmond Morris's "Emotion: Body Language"), facial expressions are largely the same across cultures. Why do you think there is great cultural variability in body language but little or no cultural variability in facial expressions?

MULTIPLE-CHOICE ITEMS

1. The fact that human facial expressions for various emotions mirror those made by chimpanzees suggests that
   a. cultural factors dictate the form that facial expressions take.
   b. cultural factors eliminate variation in the form of facial expressions.
   c. some aspects of facial expressions have a biological basis.
   d. the emotional sophistication of chimpanzees has been vastly underestimated.

2. Which of the following facial expressions is associated with aggression in primates?
   a. tightness in the mouth
   b. lowered eyebrows
   c. Both a and b
   d. Neither a nor b

3. Which of the following facial expressions is associated with fear or submissiveness in primates?
   a. baring of the teeth
   b. pursed lips
   c. Both a and b
   d. Neither a nor b

4. Smiling appears to have evolved from facial expressions used to signal
   a. aggression.
   b. surprise.
   c. fear.
   d. disgust.

5. According to the video, the capacity for facial expressions evolved from
   a. the need to communicate nonverbally prior to the evolution of language.
   b. the need to communicate nonverbally; talking aloud might have scared away prey or alerted enemies or predators to one's location.
   c. the need to form cultural groups to aid survival.
   d. the practical value of facial muscles to aid eating.

9.3 Emotion: Body Language

Normally when we think of scientific research, we imagine people in white laboratory coats carrying clipboards and examining test tubes in windowless rooms bathed in fluorescent light. There are, of course, other ways of doing research, as exemplified in this video. Desmond Morris, a self-described "man watcher," spends his time out in the real world examining how real people behave in interactions with other real people. There are no subjects or confederates, and he does not manipulate independent variables, as is common in research that takes place within the laboratory. In this video, Dr. Morris describes some of his work in demonstrating the wide cultural variation in gestures that people use to greet and communicate with one another.

TIPS

- Don't fall into the trap of finding the physical gestures of another culture comical, amusing, or silly. Think about how someone from another culture might view our greeting rituals as strange.
- Travel-oriented Web sites are good places to search for information regarding what kinds of hand gestures or body movements might be considered offensive in another culture. Non-Western countries are a good place to look for differences.
- After watching this video, be sure to look at the video called "Language of the Face" (see Activity 9.2). In it Dr. Morris describes some aspects of facial expressions that are culturally universal and explains how they are related to facial expressions in other primates.

REFLECTION QUESTION

The "foot touching head" greeting shown in the video may seem bizarre to our Western sensibilities, but it's probably no stranger than our own greetings. To gain a feeling for variation in our own culture, ask your parents how they greeted one another when they were young, and compare it to how young people greet one another today. Why do you think greeting rituals have changed? Do these changes reflect anything about variation in youth culture or society in general?

MULTIPLE-CHOICE ITEMS

1. At the outset of his research, Dr. Morris strove to
   a. catalog genetic variation in facial expressions.
   b. catalog genetic variation in bodily gestures.
   c. create a "dictionary" of human body language.
   d. learn how nonverbal human communication is similar to the way birds and other animals communicate with one another.

2. Greeting gestures like shaking hands can either be egalitarian (e.g., the behavior of both parties is similar) or status conscious (e.g., the behavior of a lower-status person is clearly distinguished from that of a higher-status person). Dr. Morris found that greeting gestures
   a. used to be more egalitarian than they are today.
   b. used to be more status conscious than they are today.
   c. have varied little over historical time periods in terms of egalitarianism.
   d. shift dramatically in terms of egalitarianism several times a century.

3. Which of the following statements about cultural variation in hand gestures is true?
   a. Hand gestures do not vary much across cultures.
   b. Hand gestures vary a great deal across cultures, but there is little chance for confusion, since there is little overlap.
   c. Hand gestures vary a great deal across cultures, but there is little chance for confusion, because the meanings of these gestures are so closely tied to the physical appearance of the gestures.
   d. Hand gestures vary a great deal across cultures; often the same gesture can mean vastly different things in different countries.

4. Dr. Morris's approach to studying behavior can best be described as
   a. observational.
   b. experimental.
   c. statistical.
   d. hypothetical.

5. Eileen is traveling in the South of France. She stops to ask for directions. After speaking with a local person, she asks him how her French is. He does not say anything. Instead he gestures, making a circle with his index finger and thumb and his other fingers splayed out above the index finger. The man's gesture indicates that he thinks Eileen's French is
   a. excellent.
   b. very good.
   c. okay.
   d. worthless.

9.4 Detection of Deception

Imagine you come home to find that the leftover pizza you planned to eat for dinner has disappeared from the refrigerator. It must have been your roommate. No one else could have taken the pizza, but when you ask, your roommate denies it. This has to be a lie, but how can you be sure? Unfortunately, there is no way to be sure. Polygraph tests rely on physiological measures to detect dishonesty. In general, these tests are not reliable; the results of polygraph tests are generally not admissible in court. But psychologists are starting to use neuropsychological measures to distinguish truth from dishonesty. These measures are a long way from being able to detect lying with precision, but as you will see in this activity, they are showing a great deal of promise.

TIPS

- After finishing the video, go back and review the beginning to see if you can guess which of the people in the three initial videos are lying.

- Ask your roommates a series of simple questions. Instruct your roommate to vary whether or he or she answers the questions honestly. Is it easier to detect honesty live or on the computer screen? Do you think that knowing your roommate helps you detect dishonesty?

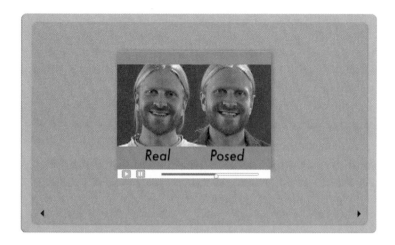

REFLECTION QUESTION

Can we be sure that someone is telling the truth by examining his or her facial expression? Why or why not? What is one area of the face that looks different when a person is exhibiting a real smile versus a posed smile? Why? What is one area of the face that does not look different when a person is genuinely smiling or faking a smile? Why? Be sure to discuss both the brain regions and the facial muscles involved in the process.

MULTIPLE-CHOICE ITEMS

1. When a person is really smiling, the _____ controls the action of the smile.
   a. hippocampus
   b. cortex
   c. limbic system
   d. pons

2. If you want to determine if Cathy is genuinely smiling, you should focus on her
   a. eyes.
   b. mouth.
   c. eyes and mouth.
   d. eyes, mouth, and neck.

3. The zygomatic muscle, which manipulates movement around the mouth, can be controlled by
   a. the limbic system only.
   b. the cortex only.
   c. both the limbic system and the cortex.
   d. neither the limbic system nor the cortex.

CONTINUED FROM PAGE 117

4. The orbicularis muscle around the eyes is controlled by the part of the brain that oversees
   a. genuine smiles.
   b. posed smiles.
   c. both genuine and posed smiles.
   d. neither genuine nor posed smiles.

5. The new technologies that have been developed to detect deception
   a. have been rather unsuccessful, producing lots of errors.
   b. are capable of detecting deception about 50 percent of the time.
   c. are quite accurate in discriminating liars from truth tellers.
   d. can pinpoint the moment that a person begins to lie.

Sexuality and Gender

10.1 Gender Stereotypes: Implicit Associations Test

Would you be more surprised if the professor of your English literature class was a woman or a man? What about your chemistry professor or engineering professor or psychology professor? When questioned directly, most people from Western societies would respond that a professor is just as likely to be a man as a woman. This is because most Westerners hold an egalitarian view of gender roles in society; that is, anything a man can do a woman can do just as well. Although this is the prevailing attitude when people are questioned directly, it is possible that many or perhaps most people still harbor some latent stereotypes about how women and men are "supposed" to behave. The current activity was designed to evaluate your latent gender stereotypes by asking you to categorize lists of words comprising both gender-specific and gender-neutral words.

TIPS

- Before starting the activity, think about your honest attitudes toward gender stereotypes. Do you really think that men and women are equal, or do you think that each gender has particular strengths and weaknesses? Be honest with yourself so that you can compare your beliefs about your attitudes with the outcome of the word-categorization test.

- Work quickly but carefully. It is very important to avoid mistakes, because these will inflate your response times.

- Do not panic if the results of the test suggest that you possess latent gender stereotypes. Most people show some evidence of these kinds of unconscious inclinations, and your behavior in the real world is much more important than the way you respond on this kind of laboratory test.

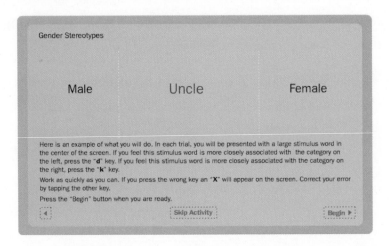

REFLECTION QUESTION

Many people consciously hold egalitarian attitudes about gender but will demonstrate gender stereotyping on a task similar to the one you just completed. That is, their expressed attitudes won't match their responses on the task. Why do you think this is? Do you think your results accurately reflect your beliefs? Why or why not?

MULTIPLE-CHOICE ITEMS

1. A set of expectations that defines what is appropriate behavior for men and women is called a
   a. gender bias.
   b. gender role.
   c. gender stereotype.
   d. gender asymmetry.

2. Laura assumes that Andrew must love sports because he is a man. Laura is expressing a
   a. gender asymmetry.
   b. gender stereotype.
   c. gender discrimination.
   d. gender prototype.

3. Gender roles
   a. are remarkably similar across cultures.
   b. vary from culture to culture.
   c. exist only for women.
   d. exist only for men.

4. Jack believes that women are more likely to be associated with domestic chores than men. Which of the following is true?
   a. Jack's belief reflects what men believe but not what women believe.
   b. Jack's belief reflects what women believe but not what men believe.
   c. Jack's belief reflects what most men and most women believe.
   d. Jack's belief is atypical. Most men and women do not share this belief.

5. Stereotypes about men and women
   a. have shifted dramatically over the last century.
   b. are indistinguishable from each other.
   c. have changed very little over the last century.
   d. have been greatly affected by the feminist movement of the last forty years.

10.2 Sexual Response: Masters and Johnson

Freud is often considered a pioneer regarding the unconscious, psychological processes associated with human sexuality. William Masters and Virginia Johnson are often considered pioneers in studying the physiological processes associated with human sexuality. The goal of their research was to apply the scientific method to evaluate many commonly held beliefs regarding sexuality. What made their research groundbreaking was the social context in which they worked. Sexuality was not a topic that was then discussed in polite company. Indeed, as you will learn in this video, Masters began by studying prostitutes, presumably because he believed they would be more open to discussing their sexual behavior. The researchers also met with a great deal of resistance from the medical community, not only because of their subject matter but because of their methods and conclusions as well. However, Masters and Johnson's research formed the foundation of our current understanding of the physiology of human sexuality.

TIPS

- Some of the images in this video are graphic, so be prepared. As you watch, remember that these images were initially recorded approximately fifty years ago. However you might respond to these videos, they would have been much more shocking at the time they were recorded.

- As you watch the video, think about some of the facts that Masters and Johnson discovered. Many will seem obvious to you, but it was their research that made us aware of many facts about sexuality that are now viewed as common knowledge.

 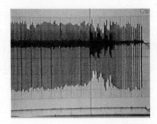 

REFLECTION QUESTION

As the video makes clear, social norms regarding open discussion of sexual behavior have changed dramatically over the last half-century. How do you think the work of Masters and Johnson influenced that social change? What might current norms be like if this work had never been conducted or published? Do you think their work might have influenced broader political initiatives like the women's rights movement?

MULTIPLE-CHOICE ITEMS

1. Dr. Masters embarked on his research to
   a. establish a scientific understanding of the sexual organs to match our scientific understanding of other organs (e.g., heart, lungs, brain).
   b. help his patients achieve more satisfying sex lives.
   c. counteract religious leaders' teachings regarding sex.
   d. overcome his own difficulties in talking about sex with his patients.

2. Which of the following was *not* one of the stages of sexual response identified by Masters and Johnson's research?
   a. foreplay
   b. excitement
   c. plateau
   d. resolution

3. What was one of the barriers that made it difficult for Masters and Johnson to publish their research in medical journals?
   a. a relatively small amount of data
   b. resistance to publishing their data because of the subject matter
   c. Both a and b
   d. Neither a nor b

4. Masters began collaborating with Johnson because
   a. of her outstanding medical training.
   b. of her experience studying sexual response.
   c. she was a prostitute and therefore more sexually experienced than he was.
   d. she was a woman who would be better able to interview female research subjects.

5. According to the video, Masters and Johnson's research had a greater impact than any other research on the attitudes and/or behavior of
   a. the medical community.
   b. the religious community.
   c. the legal/political community.
   d. "regular" people.

10.3 Sex and Medicine:
Sex, Sin, and Sickness

Modern society often looks to science to cure its ills. For example, many look to scientific innovation as a way to combat global warming. But science is not a magical cure-all. It is flawed, because the practitioners of scientific investigations are also flawed. This video demonstrates some of the fallacies that have been promulgated when the scientific method has been applied to the study of human sexuality. Alternatively, one might describe this video as demonstrating the fallacies promulgated when the scientific method was applied in an attempt to *control* human sexuality. One might argue that the conclusions reached by these scientists were weak because they did not begin with an objective agenda. Instead, they tried to use science to further religious or other social ideals related to sexual behavior.

TIPS

- How is that intelligent people can come to believe that something like diet can make one more or less prone to engage in masturbation? What are some common beliefs today that you think are likely to be proven wrong by subsequent generations of scientific inquiry?

- If you find yourself frustrated by an inability to distinguish fact from fiction, try doing an Internet search using the term *skeptic*. There are many groups of skeptics, most of whom are devoted to using scientific data and reasoning to approach important political, social, religious, and scientific questions.

REFLECTION QUESTION

We often think of scientific research as being an objective search for the truth. We accept that the conclusions a scientist reaches must be unaffected by political or religious views. Does the evidence suggest that this was the case regarding early scientific studies of human sexuality? Do you think that scientific research today is free from political or religious influence?

MULTIPLE-CHOICE ITEMS

1. During the Middle Ages, medical work on human sexuality
   a. sought to undermine the church's teachings.
   b. sought to confirm the church's teachings.
   c. proceeded independently of church doctrine.
   d. carefully studied the sexual behavior of the clergy.

2. Dr. Atisso's work
   a. indicated that masturbation was a normal part of most healthy adults' sex lives.
   b. indicated that masturbation had negative medical consequences, including madness.
   c. laid the foundation for Alfred Kinsey's work several centuries later.
   d. laid the foundation for Masters and Johnson's work several centuries later.

3. At one time, the scientific community believed that a woman who
   a. masturbated was mentally ill.
   b. had sexual intercourse after menopause was mentally ill.
   c. Both a and b were considered evidence of mental illness.
   d. Neither a nor b was considered evidence of mental illness.

4. Surgical treatments to "cure" one of the desire to masturbate
   a. were once used for males but not for females.
   b. were once used for females but not for males.
   c. were once used for both males and females.
   d. were never used for either males or females.

5. One of the most outrageous scientific approaches to curing people of excessive sex drives was
   a. psychoanalysis.
   b. electroshock therapy.
   c. starvation.
   d. bland breakfast cereal.

10.4 Sex and Medicine: Alfred Kinsey

Like many individuals who made significant contributions to psychology (Freud being just one example), Alfred Kinsey was not trained as a psychologist. He was a biologist who had studied wasps for the first half of his career. This video will describe how Kinsey became interested in human sexuality and how he approached its study. Note how Kinsey's student describes how Kinsey believed that studying sexual behavior in humans was fundamentally the same as studying the behavior of wasps. Each posed an interesting set of research questions that could best be answered by applying the scientific method. This view may seem entirely appropriate to you now, but bear in mind that Kinsey was working in the first half of the twentieth century. To equate human behavior, particularly sexual behavior, with animal behavior was revolutionary and controversial at that time. Thus, it is not surprising that Kinsey's work faced a great deal of resistance, both from within and outside of the scientific community.

TIPS

- Compare the sexual knowledge of the college students (now senior citizens) interviewed in the video with the sexual knowledge of most college students today.

- Note that Kinsey's goal was to find as much variation as he could in sexual behavior. This might seem at odds with the standard view that the goal of psychological science is to find regularity in behavior. However, Kinsey used the variability that he found to try to decide what were the natural boundaries in sexual behavior, so that regularity could be found within those boundaries.

- Kinsey's work was the subject of a recent movie, called *Kinsey*. It might be worth viewing this film to see how Hollywood presents the life and work of this pioneering researcher.

 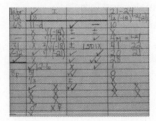 

REFLECTION QUESTION

Kinsey approached the study of sexual behavior as a scientific question. In so doing, he demystified human sexuality. He tried to remove its taboo status, likening sexual behavior to other kinds of human behavior considered normal, such as eating, drinking, or sleeping. What would you think to be the long-term benefits of Kinsey's work to demystify human sexuality? Do you think there were any negative consequences of eliminating the taboo of discussing sexuality in public?

MULTIPLE-CHOICE ITEMS

1. Kinsey began to research human sexuality
   a. to compare human sexual behavior with wasp sexual behavior.
   b. to compare human behavior with chimpanzee sexual behavior.
   c. because he thought social taboos regarding the discussion of sexual behavior were destructive.
   d. because he was stunned by the lack of scientific knowledge on the subject.

2. The majority of Kinsey's research was conducted using
   a. prostitutes.
   b. college students.
   c. government employees.
   d. a broad cross section of the population.

3. Unlike Masters and Johnson's research, Kinsey's
   a. collected detailed physiological responses from his subjects.
   b. collected detailed case studies of his subjects' behavior.
   c. was not interested in everyday sexual behavior.
   d. was based on the idea that his subjects lacked sufficient vocabulary to communicate about sex effectively.

4. Kinsey's work relied on case studies, so his research could best be described as
   a. observational.
   b. experimental.
   c. cognitive.
   d. neurobiological.

5. Kinsey's marriage course was popular because
   a. it provided more up-to-date research than other similar courses of his era.
   b. it was the first college course that included frank discussions of sexual behavior.
   c. he was a notoriously easy grader.
   d. students love professors who wear bow ties.

10.5 Biological Aspects
of Sexuality: Sexual Identity

How does an embryo become a son or daughter, a brother or sister, a mother or father? Gender identity is influenced by a complex set of factors working together. Part of our gender identity comes from biology through the action of chromosomes at conception and hormones that are released while we are still in the womb. The biological component of gender identity is often referred to as a person's sex. Part of our gender identity comes from social expectations and the way we are raised by our parents. Thus, there is a great deal of variability in how gender is expressed across individuals. These videos demonstrate some of this variability, although what you will see and what you have most likely encountered in your life is a small fraction of the total range of variability in sexual identity that exists in the world.

TIP

- As you watch the videos, think about ways that your own behavior compares with the most rigid views of what is or is not appropriate for males and females in our society.

REFLECTION QUESTION

In the "Changing Genders" video, Angela describes a loss of interest in previous hobbies. It is implied that the change is a result of hormonal or psychodynamic factors. Try to think of other explanations for the observed change in interests.

MULTIPLE-CHOICE ITEMS

1. A child's sex is determined by
   a. the combined action of several genes.
   b. a single chromosome.
   c. environmental factors at the time of conception.
   d. environmental factors several weeks after conception.

2. Which of the following statements about the process of sex differentiation is true?
   a. The process of sex differentiation has been well understood for many years.
   b. The process of sex differentiation is remarkably similar across animal species.
   c. The process of sex differentiation generally leaves a child on either one or another end of a continuum from male to female.
   d. The process of sex differentiation is strongly affected by cultural expectations.

3. The case of David/Angela suggests that
   a. gender identity is complex and not as simple as male versus female.
   b. transitioning from one gender identity to another is a straightforward process.
   c. men and women cannot share interests in the same hobbies.
   d. gender stereotypes are more accurate than we might want to believe.

4. The research described in the first video suggests that gender-role confusion
   a. is an example of psychological pathology.
   b. must be determined by psychological factors.
   c. must be determined by environmental factors.
   d. may be determined by biological factors.

10.6 Adolescence: Sexual Identity

Along with all of the other identity work that goes on during adolescence, teenagers wrestle with their attitudes about sexual identity and sexual behavior. The videos collected here present a variety of views on the issues that must be faced when struggling to determine one's sexual identity. Developing a sense of one's own sexual identity is not simple, nor is it an endpoint. Many life decisions and many of the experiences we have are direct consequences of how the search for sexual identity proceeds. Thus, these videos describe the processes involved in developing a sense of sexual identity for both heterosexual and nonheterosexual adolescents. They also discuss how sexual identities influence behaviors in other areas of life, both in adolescence and into adulthood.

TIP

- As you watch the videos, take careful note of how the issues related to sexual identity differ across the different kinds of sexual identities. Note where there are similarities and where there are differences. Think about how these issues might have affected the development of your own sexual identity.

Several of the videos that you watched suggest that understanding the development of sexual identity, and minority sexual identity in particular, requires an understanding of the historical context. What major trends have been observed, and how have these trends influenced the process of "coming out" in the United States today? In what ways does the current social climate inhibit the freedom to explore sexuality?

MULTIPLE-CHOICE ITEMS

1. According to Kim Rice, the primary concern of LGBT (lesbian, gay, bisexual, and transgender) youth with respect to sexual identity is a
   a. fear of contracting sexually transmitted infections.
   b. fear of feeling different.
   c. fear of failing to find or maintain a romantic relationship.
   d. fear of pregnancy.

2. The process of developing a sexual identity is typically initiated during
   a. adolescence but completed before adolescence ends.
   b. adolescence but lasts throughout the life span.
   c. childhood but is completed before adolescence ends.
   d. childhood but lasts throughout the life span.

3. Coming out
   a. occurs as soon as one engages in same-sex activity.
   b. occurs as soon as one experiences same-sex fantasies.
   c. is not a central component of one's personal identity.
   d. is a public affirmation of same-sex behavior.

4. Sexual-minority youth are coming out earlier now than they have in the past. One might attribute this change in behavior to
   a. changes in the legal consequences of identifying oneself as nonheterosexual.
   b. changes in the psychological assessment of being nonheterosexual.
   c. changes in the social implications of identifying oneself as nonheterosexual.
   d. All of the above

10.7 Sexual Response: Viagra

Viagra, a common drug prescribed to treat sexual dysfunction, was discovered more or less by accident. Patients who had been taking a drug to combat vascular disease reported an increase in sexual arousal. In addition to tracing the history of Viagra, this video also discusses treatments for female sexual dysfunction. Interestingly, Viagra has not proven effective with women, but treatment with testosterone, which is usually considered a male sex hormone, has shown some effectiveness. This discovery underscores some of the differences between male and female sexual responses.

TIP

- Accidental scientific discoveries are common in medical science, as well as science in general. A quick Internet search will uncover many examples of modern-day miracles where luck played an important role. Of course, luck is never enough; it takes a clever scientist to recognize a pattern as significant rather than irrelevant. For example, if the researchers investigating Viagra as a cure for vascular disease had considered the sexual arousal of their subjects to be a nuisance, this drug would not be available for males suffering from sexual dysfunction today.

 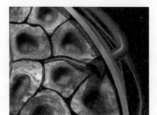 

The gentleman in the video claims that using Viagra has made him feel like a "whole complete human being, again, which is something that I haven't felt like for quite a long period of time." What does this quote suggest about the place of sexual function and sexual identity in one's larger sense of self? Think about what other kinds of disabilities or dysfunctions might have a similar impact on one's sense of self.

MULTIPLE-CHOICE ITEMS

1. The discovery of Viagra was
   a. the result of years of concentrated effort by a team of researchers at Pfizer who were determined to create a drug to fight impotence.
   b. accidental; the drug was originally designed to fight high blood pressure.
   c. accidental; the drug was originally designed to fight vascular disease.
   d. an example of unethical practices in biomedical research.

2. The fact that drugs can have such a pronounced impact on sexual behavior indicates that sexual problems can often be attributed to
   a. environmental factors.
   b. psychological factors.
   c. psychodynamic factors.
   d. physical factors.

3. Viagra seems to work by
   a. increasing blood flow to the penis.
   b. relaxing muscles in the penis.
   c. Neither a nor b
   d. Both a and b

4. Testosterone has been used as an effective means of rekindling sexual desire in
   a. men.
   b. women.
   c. both men and women.
   d. neither men nor women.

5. Testosterone therapy appears to work by
   a. replacing estrogen, which is naturally lost through the aging process.
   b. replacing testosterone, which is naturally lost through the aging process.
   c. a placebo effect.
   d. reducing anxiety about sexual performance.

10.8 The Science of Sexuality: Evolutionary Psychology and Mate Selection

Donald Trump is twenty-four years older than his wife, Melania. Harrison Ford is twenty-two years older than Calista Flockhart. In Hollywood, and our society in general, it is more common to see older men dating younger women than the reverse (although Demi Moore is fifteen years older than Ashton Kutcher). Is this a coincidence? Evolutionary psychologists do not think so. They believe that what we find attractive is subject to natural selection, just like many of our other traits. As you will see in these videos, there is fairly strong evidence to support this view. One particularly strong line of evidence is described in the so-called waist-to-hip ratio video. This is not to say that *all* of our mate preferences are biologically determined. There are cultural shifts and cultural differences in preferred weight or hairstyles, but many of the core attributes that we value in a mate are those that increase the likelihood that our genes will be passed on to the next generation.

TIPS

- As you watch the videos, try to determine why older men tend to be attracted to younger women and vice versa. In other words, what do evolutionary psychologists think that younger women or older men offer one another in terms of reproductive fitness?

- Note that the couples given above are just examples. One cannot build a scientific argument based on a small number of examples from personal experience. As you watch the videos, pay attention to the kinds of evidence these researchers collected to support their theories. How do they exclude cultural-learning explanations for their findings?

REFLECTION QUESTION

Most people do not react to meeting potential boyfriends or girlfriends by saying to themselves, "Mmm-hmm, this person looks fertile," or even "I really think this person is going to ensure that my genes are going to be passed on to the next generation." Why do you think the powerful forces that appear to drive mate selection occur below the level of consciousness? Why are we not keenly aware of the waist-to-hip ratio or the likely fertility of a potential mate? Is it because humans engage in a great deal of sexual activity that is not directed toward producing offspring, or are other factors important?

MULTIPLE-CHOICE ITEMS

1. Men tend to prefer younger women because younger women tend to
   a. have more resources.
   b. live longer.
   c. be more fertile.
   d. be less independent.

2. Women tend to prefer older men because older men tend to
   a. have more resources.
   b. live longer.
   c. be more fertile.
   d. be less independent.

3. Evolutionary psychologists believe that the mate-selection preferences of men and women are the result of natural selection. Which of the following is considered evidence that supports this view?
   a. Mate-selection preferences vary a great deal over human history.
   b. Mate-selection preferences vary a great deal across cultures.
   c. Mate-selection preferences are largely the same across different cultures.
   d. Mate-selection preferences are largely the same across different species of animals.

4. Which of the following statements about the waist-to-hip ratio is true?
   a. All men prefer women with a low waist-to-hip ratio.
   b. All lesbian women prefer women with a low waist-to-hip ratio.
   c. In general, women with a low waist-to-hip ratio tend to be less healthy and less able to bear children.
   d. In general, women with a low waist-to-hip ratio tend to be healthier and more able to bear children.

5. According to the video, the waist-to-hip ratio is
   a. less important than overall weight for determining female attractiveness.
   b. less important than facial attractiveness for determining female attractiveness.
   c. strongly associated with exposure to Western society's movies, magazines, and television programs.
   d. a preference that has been observed in only the last 100 to 200 years.

10.9 Adulthood: Interracial Relationships

People who are involved in interracial relationships face all of the same issues faced by people in single-race relationships, but they must also deal with additional stresses from a variety of sources. You can probably anticipate some of these sources, but others are likely to surprise you, particularly if you are not familiar with or have not been involved in an interracial relationship.

TIPS

- Dr. LaTaillade describes some of her research on interracial relationships. Think about how well the theories derived from her research capture the experiences of the interracial couples in the other videos.

- The couples represented in these videos span a fairly wide range of ages. Think about how the issues faced by the younger couple vary from those discussed by the older couple. How would you explain these differences?

Maria describes her experiences as a part of an interracial couple with James. She also describes the experiences of her parents' interracial relationship. How do Maria's experiences differ from those of her parents? What do you think explains this difference: antidiscrimination legislation? multicultural awareness? changes in social norms regarding openness and freedom of expression? Do you think people's attitudes have changed, or are people simply less willing to demonstrate overt prejudice?

MULTIPLE-CHOICE ITEMS

1. According to Dr. LaTaillade, interracial couples face the most overt discrimination from
    a. strangers they meet in public.
    b. public institutions like the government.
    c. private institutions (e.g., landlords refusing housing).
    d. friends and family.

2. According to Dr. LaTaillade, interracial couples face the most covert discrimination from
    a. strangers they meet in public.
    b. public institutions like the government.
    c. private institutions (e.g., landlords refusing housing).
    d. friends and family.

3. The experiences described by Richard and Alexis are consistent with the research described by Dr. LaTaillade in that they have experienced the most
    a. overt discrimination from strangers they meet in public.
    b. covert discrimination from strangers they meet in public.
    c. overt discrimination from friends and family.
    d. covert discrimination from friends and family.

4. Maria explains that her family's resistance to her interracial relationship
    a. primarily reflected her family's prejudice.
    b. was in part due to conflicts created by the different cultural expectations of her background.
    c. Both a and b
    d. Neither a nor b

ELEVEN

Development

11.1 Understanding Nature and Nurture

Although conversations about the effects of genes and the environment often turn into either-or debates, it is important to remember that nature *and* nurture combine to affect most human traits and behaviors. Genes tend to set a range of values. A 5 foot 7 inch male and a 5 foot 4 inch female are unlikely to have a child who will be 6 feet tall. But these parents can influence the height of their child by ensuring a healthy environment that includes a well-balanced diet, plenty of sleep, and good exercise. Of course, it is difficult to observe the effects of genes and the environment on human characteristics; for obvious ethical reasons, researchers can't control the genes and environments of large numbers of babies. This activity is designed to allow you to produce a large data set of virtual babies with varying genetic endowments and childhood environments. The IQs of these virtual babies will demonstrate how nature and nurture influence intelligence.

TIPS

- Although it will become a little repetitive, you should produce a data set of approximately twenty-four babies. This should not take too long and will allow you enough data to appreciate the pattern and answer the questions that follow the activity.

- When generating your virtual babies, make sure you create several using each set of parents and every type of environment. Again, the more variability you generate in your virtual babies, the easier it will be for you to identify a pattern in their IQ scores.

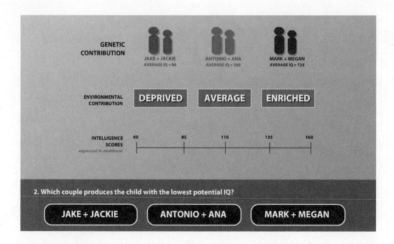

REFLECTION QUESTION

Judit Polgar's experiences are not unique. There are many cases in which a father tried to develop his child into a star by controlling every aspect of the child's environment. Recent cases in the field of athletics are Serena and Venus Williams, who have become world-class tennis players, and Todd Marinovich, whose success as a football player is debatable. Use the Internet to read about Marinovich and his experiences. What does this case tell you about how easy or difficult it is to control someone's behavior by manipulating her or his environment?

MULTIPLE-CHOICE ITEMS

1. Polgar's parents, grandparents, and siblings are highly intelligent. This fact suggests that her chess ability is a function of
   a. her genes.
   b. her environment.
   c. neither her genes nor her environment.
   d. both her genes and her environment.

2. Polgar's father spent countless hours training her to be a great chess player. This fact suggests that her chess ability is a function of
   a. her genes.
   b. her environment.
   c. neither her genes nor her environment.
   d. both her genes and her environment.

3. For any physical or intellectual trait, the reaction range refers to the range of
   a. environments that an individual is likely to experience.
   b. environments that an individual actually experiences.
   c. outcomes that are possible, with the actual outcome depending on the quality of the environment that the individual experiences.
   d. outcomes that are possible, depending on factors in addition to genes and the environment.

4. The reaction range is determined by
   a. genes, but where one falls within the range is determined by the environment.
   b. the environment, but where one falls within the range is determined by one's genes.
   c. factors that are poorly understood.
   d. how one reacts to one's environment.

5. Susie has tall parents. Kara has short parents. Susie and Kara are most likely to be the same height if
   a. Susie receives a highly nutritious diet and Kara receives a poor diet.
   b. Susie receives a poor diet and Kara receives a highly nutritious diet.
   c. Susie and Kara both receive highly nutritious diets.
   d. Susie and Kara both receive poor diets.

11.2 Genes and Behavior: Twin Studies

The tension between nature and nurture is often presented as a dichotomy: our behavior is *either* determined by our genes *or* it is produced by the environment in which we developed. Most researchers do not believe that either the genes or the environment can fully explain most complex human behaviors. Instead, genes and the environment work together in complex ways to establish who we are and how we behave. For ethical reasons, it is difficult to run controlled studies examining how genes and the environment work on shaping human behavior, because these kinds of experiments would involve either genetically modifying humans at some stage during their development or randomly assigning children to be raised in deliberately impoverished or enriched environments.

One ethical way to study genes and the environment is to study twins. Identical twins share the exact same set of genes, so the effects of the environment can be seen by examining differences in abilities or personalities. Some research programs look at twins who were separated at birth and reared apart. Others, like the one described in this video, compare twins who were raised together. As the video will demonstrate, regardless of how the studies are conducted, the data clearly show the complex interaction of genes and the environment.

TIPS

- Note that the video makes an analogy between physical attributes like height and mental attributes like intelligence. Just as the height or athletic ability of a child are likely to be similar to those of the parents, so are mental abilities and personality traits.

- Bear in mind that genes are not the whole story. Two professional athletes will not necessarily give birth to a future professional athlete. Note how the relative IQ scores of the identical twins in the video varied as they grew older.

REFLECTION QUESTION

It would not be terribly controversial if, during a campaign speech, a political candidate claimed that height is largely controlled by genetic factors. However, a great deal of controversy would likely erupt if the same candidate in the same speech claimed that intelligence is largely controlled by genetic factors. What are the political or societal issues that cause the second, but not the first, claim to be controversial?

MULTIPLE-CHOICE ITEMS

1. Identical twins
   a. occur when two eggs are fertilized simultaneously.
   b. occur when a single fertilized egg splits during development.
   c. do not have to be the same gender.
   d. are no more similar genetically than fraternal twins.

2. Eric is larger than his identical twin brother Corey because
   a. Eric received more food than his brother while they were in the womb.
   b. Eric received more genetic material from his father than Corey did.
   c. Eric received more genetic material from his mother than Corey did.
   d. their parents loved Eric more.

3. Eric and Corey differ in terms of their
   a. physical and psychological attributes.
   b. physical and intellectual attributes.
   c. physical and emotional attributes.
   d. physical attributes only.

4. The fact that Eric initially scored better on IQ tests than Corey did demonstrates that
   a. genes affect intelligence.
   b. the environment affects intelligence.
   c. both genes and the environment affect intelligence.
   d. neither genes nor the environment affect intelligence.

5. The fact that the gap between the twins closed as they grew older shows that
   a. genes affect intelligence.
   b. the environment affects intelligence.
   c. both genes and the environment affect intelligence.
   d. neither genes nor the environment affect intelligence.

11.3 Infant Vision: Seeing through the Eyes of a Child

William James, one of the fathers of modern psychology (and Henry's brother), described an infant's world as a "booming, buzzing confusion." Since James made this claim, a great deal of research has demonstrated that infants and very young children engage in purposeful behavior and have the ability to perceive many aspects of their physical environment clearly. This is not to say that infants perceive the world the same way as adults do. This activity will give you an opportunity to see the world the way infants see it at various stages of their development.

TIPS

- Of course, we cannot ask preverbal infants how they see the world or what they see. The simulations in this activity are based on many experiments that have been conducted to determine whether infants can detect a change in a visual scene (like changing its color). An infant who detects a change in a visual scene will tend to look at the changed scene longer than a baby who does not notice the change.

- One might expect an infant's visual perception to be better developed from birth than it is. Can you think of an evolutionary explanation for why infant vision is relatively poor at birth?

REFLECTION QUESTION

People often react to newborns in ways that assume the infant can see like an adult (e.g., playing peekaboo with a newborn from across the room). How might you educate new parents on their newborn's visual abilities? What would you tell them about their newborn's vision? their 1-month-old's vision? their 6-month-old's vision? What tips would you give them regarding playing with their infant at each of these ages that would be visually appropriate for the child?

MULTIPLE-CHOICE ITEMS

1. A newborn
   a. cannot see anything.
   b. can see objects only a few inches away.
   c. can see objects about one foot away.
   d. can see objects several feet away.

2. Baby Suzanna is 2 months old. Her mom places a red block about one foot in front of her. Suzanna most likely
   a. cannot see the object at that distance.
   b. can see the object but cannot distinguish its color.
   c. can see the object and distinguish its color.
   d. can see the object and recognize its dimensionality.

3. At 1 year, a baby's visual sensitivity is _____ times greater than it was at birth.
   a. two
   b. four
   c. six
   d. eight

4. Five-month-old Derek is now able to
   a. discriminate between a picture of a flower and a real flower.
   b. see his mother's face when she is holding him.
   c. discriminate between a blue rattle and a pink rattle.
   d. All of the above

5. Visual abilities in infants
   a. expand rapidly after birth.
   b. do not improve until about 6 months of age.
   c. are quite sensitive at birth.
   d. decline in the first two months, then expand rapidly.

11.4 Cognitive Development: Categorization

Little Suzie takes a rubber ball and throws it across the living room. Her parents cheer and praise her efforts. Suzie then grabs a glass ball from the Christmas tree and throws it too. Her parents' reaction is significantly less positive as they scurry to clean up the broken glass before Suzie cuts herself. How did Suzie's cognitive system fail her? One might view this as a failure on Suzie's part to categorize items, to figure out how things are similar and how they are different. Both of the objects that Suzie threw were round, but whereas rubber balls retain their shape when thrown against the floor, glass balls usually do not. Thus, learning to categorize items can save a young child from having to spend too much time in time-out. It can also help them navigate their world more effectively by enabling them to predict how objects in their environment will behave and how they can be used. These videos show how children at varying ages categorize—or fail to categorize—common objects.

TIPS

- Note that in all cases the children are able to name all of the objects that they are then asked to categorize. Therefore, categorization failures cannot be attributed to a lack of familiarity with the objects.

- The important aspect of the children's behavior is not whether they correctly choose the oddball item. The explanations are much more important. A child could randomly choose the item that did not belong. The only way we know if they can categorize the items is by asking them to explain why they chose the item they did. One might argue that the youngest children understand the appropriate categories but lack the language skills to explain their choices. Can you think of any arguments against this explanation?

- Think about how Piaget might have interpreted these videos. Are they consistent with a stage model of cognitive development? Why or why not?

These videos were made for demonstration purposes, not research. What are some of the things that made these interactions unsuitable for research purposes? In other words, did the way the researchers interacted with the children make it hard to know how much the children really understood? How might you design the interactions differently to avoid this kind of confusion? Would eliminating all researcher–child interactions be a good idea, or might these raise additional problems?

MULTIPLE-CHOICE ITEMS

1. Caroline
   a. selected the wrong item.
   b. selected the right item but was unable to explain why she chose it.
   c. selected the right item but provided an illogical explanation.
   d. was unable to select an item.

2. These videos suggest that 4-year-old children
   a. are incapable of categorizing items based only on physical appearance.
   b. are capable of categorizing items based only on physical appearance.
   c. lack the vocabulary to complete a categorization task.
   d. None of the above

3. These videos suggest that children under the age of 7
   a. have the cognitive ability to categorize items but lack the vocabulary to do so.
   b. lack the cognitive ability to categorize items, although they possess the vocabulary to do so.
   c. lack both the cognitive ability to categorize items and the vocabulary to do so.
   d. None of the above

11.5 Conservation

A persistent question in developmental psychology is whether the cognitive changes that occur across childhood are *quantitative* or *qualitative*. A quantitative change would suggest that young children possess the same cognitive skills as adults but a reduced capacity for using these skills. A qualitative change would imply that children lack certain skills early in life but develop them sequentially in stages as they grow and learn. Jean Piaget was a strong proponent of the belief that cognitive changes were qualitative in nature. He developed a series of cognitive tests—appropriate for preverbal and verbal children alike—to test his ideas. This video will demonstrate three of the cognitive skills that Piaget believed children acquire as they mature: *object permanence, egocentrism,* and *conservation*. The video also demonstrates the kinds of experimental methods that Piaget used to test whether children had acquired these skills. Still, Piaget's work is considered one of the foundations of modern developmental psychology.

TIP

- Many modern developmental psychologists are not convinced that development occurs in discrete stages; rather, they believe that cognitive skills are acquired more gradually than Piaget thought. Many researchers now believe that the kinds of tests Piaget used overestimate the extent to which cognitive skills are either present or absent.

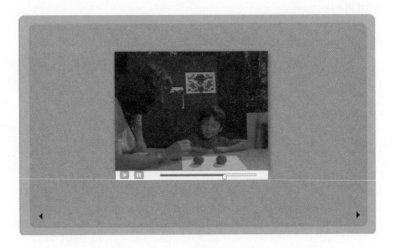

REFLECTION QUESTIONS

1. A family of four (Dad, Mom, a 7-year-old, and a 3-year-old) is getting ready to order dinner at a restaurant they frequently visit. While waiting for their waiter, Mom and Dad ask both children what they think each family member will order. According to Piaget, will the children respond similarly or differently? Why? What might an order from the 3-year-old look like? What about the 7-year-old's order?

2. At the end of the meal, everyone orders the same ice cream dessert (two scoops of vanilla). When the ice cream arrives, some of it has melted. When the bowls are passed out to the family members, the 3-year-old complains that his older sister and father have more ice cream than he does, even though they don't. Why?

MULTIPLE-CHOICE ITEMS

1. Piaget believed that a child's ability to think
   a. develops in stages.
   b. is fully developed by ages 8 to 9.
   c. is quite similar to an adult's ability to think.
   d. develops in a continuous fashion.

2. Three-year-old Leo and his mother are shopping for his father's birthday gift. When Leo is asked what he thinks his father would like, Leo responds, "A choo-choo train!" Leo is demonstrating which of Piaget's concepts?
   a. conservation
   c. egocentrism
   b. abstract thought
   d. symbolic thought

3. When Sadie's favorite toy doll is covered up with a blanket, Sadie begins to cry because she thinks it has disappeared. Sadie lacks
   a. conservation.
   c. symbolic thought.
   b. egocentrism.
   d. object permanence.

4. A child masters _____ when she understands that an object retains its quantity even if its appearance changes.
   a. object permanence
   c. conservation
   b. symbolism
   d. egocentrism

5. The _____ stage of development is marked by egocentric thought and a lack of conservation.
   a. sensorimotor
   c. concrete operational
   b. preoperational
   d. formal

11.6 Stages of Moral Development

Many of the difficult decisions we face in life can be characterized as moral dilemmas—choices between right and wrong. Sometimes the consequences of these choices are minor: Should you tell your roommate that her new dress looks awful? At other times, the consequences can be more serious: Should you tell your roommate that you saw her significant other with someone else? Most people worry about how their decisions will influence the way they are perceived by themselves or others. In other words, they worry about the content of their decisions and whether or not these decisions indicate that they are a "good" person. Lawrence Kohlberg was less interested in what choices people make than in the reasons they gave for making their choices. In this activity you will learn about Kohlberg's stage model of moral development.

TIPS

- Kohlberg's model has nothing to do with what choices a person makes (e.g., tattling on one's brother or not). Any choice can be placed in any of the three levels of moral development. Again, the moral decision one makes is less important than the reason one gives for making that decision.

- Before you listen to the various responses to Joe's "camp" dilemma, try to generate one response that you think would fall within each of the three levels of Kohlberg's theory.

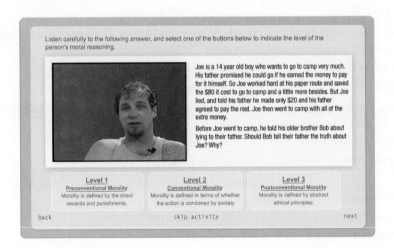

REFLECTION QUESTION

Is it ever morally acceptable to break the law? Consider driving faster than the speed limit. How might a person at each stage of moral development support the argument that it is sometimes okay to speed? How might a person at each stage of moral development support the argument that it is not okay to speed?

MULTIPLE-CHOICE ITEMS

1. Kohlberg's theory of moral development states that
    a. people pass through a fixed series of stages in moral reasoning but that many never reach the final stage of moral development.
    b. the order of stages of moral development that people pass through varies from individual to individual.
    c. although the timeline for the development of moral reasoning varies from person to person, all people eventually achieve the highest stage of development.
    d. although the order of stages of moral development varies from person to person, all people eventually experience every stage.

2. When Andy is asked why he should not lie to his parents, he responds, "Because you will get in big trouble if you are caught lying!" Billy's response reflects the_____ stage of moral development.
    a. preconventional
    b. preoperational
    c. conventional
    d. postconventional

3. Ken believes that smoking marijuana is okay because most people find it a perfectly reasonable pastime. Ken's moral reasoning is best categorized as
    a. preconventional.
    b. conventional.
    c. postconventional.
    d. postformal.

4. Camilla feels that it is all right to steal a loaf of bread if it is to save a starving person's life. She believes that human life transcends the law. Camilla is most likely in the _____ stage of moral development.
    a. conventional
    b. formal
    c. postconventional
    d. concrete

5. In the _____ stage of moral development, people judge the morality of an action in terms of whether it is acceptable to society or not.
    a. preconventional
    b. postconventional
    c. preoperational
    d. conventional

11.7 Adolescence: Adolescent Development

Conventional wisdom suggests that adolescence is a time of great intra- and interpersonal turmoil. Teenagers fight with their parents to establish their independence. They fight with one another to establish their place in their social worlds. They fight with themselves to establish their sense of identity. The videos collected here will give you an opportunity to hear how leading researchers view adolescence. Some research findings support the conventional wisdom described above, but other lines of research do not. These psychologists will also address some myths about the underlying causes of adolescent behavior. As you will see, understanding the psychological behavior of adolescents is not as simple as chalking it all up to "raging hormones."

TIPS

- These videos present the opinions of several prominent researchers in the field of adolescence. As you listen to each one, think about the ways their views differ from each other. Which psychologists attribute adolescent behavior to internal causes? Which ones attribute such behavior to external causes? Which ones stress physiological, cognitive, and emotional influences on behavior?

- It will be tempting for you to compare your own experiences with those described by these researchers. This exercise is valuable for helping you better understand the theories proposed by these researchers, but when evaluating these theories, remember that single cases are usually not enough to either accept or refute a scientific theory.

Richard Lerner, Ph.D.
Tufts University

Susan Harter, Ph.D.
Denver University

Reed Larson, Ph.D.
University of Illinois at Urbana-Champaign

REFLECTION QUESTION

How does the way these developmental experts view adolescent conflict differ from the way it is viewed in the larger community? How have these videos influenced your views on your own relationship with your parents?

MULTIPLE-CHOICE ITEMS

1. According to Dr. Larson, the relationship between emotional swings and hormone levels is
   a. significant across people. In other words, people with higher hormone levels tend to show larger mood swings.
   b. significant across time. In other words, as hormone levels increase within an individual, mood swings are more likely to be observed.
   c. more or less nonexistent. Differences in hormone levels do not predict emotional mood swings across individuals or over time.
   d. more or less what one would expect based on conventional wisdom.

2. Dr. Steinberg suggests that parent–adolescent conflict should be viewed as a
   a. negative result of raging hormones.
   b. negative result of peer influence.
   c. positive result of the media.
   d. positive result of cognitive/intellectual maturity.

3. According to Dr. Dahl, the earliest physical changes in adolescence are
   a. neuronal changes in the brain.
   b. hormonal changes signaled by the pituitary gland.
   c. hormonal changes triggered by the gonads.
   d. physiological changes in the sensory/perceptual systems.

4. The "myth of adolescence as a time of storm and stress" is that
   a. adolescent development is not synonymous with conflict or crisis.
   b. the absence of conflict should be the goal of every teenager.
   c. emotional mood swings are rarely observed during adolescence.
   d. adolescence is a time when personal identity tends to remain fairly stable.

5. Relational self-worth refers to
   a. valuing oneself based on the quality of one's relationship with others.
   b. valuing one's relations with others more than one values oneself.
   c. differing levels of self-esteem across different interpersonal contexts.
   d. differing levels of self-esteem across different emotional contexts.

11.8 Suicide Risk Factors

Reviewing the risk factors of suicide is valuable, because the incidence of suicide is higher during adolescence than at any other time of life. Recognizing the warning signs can help you determine whether you or someone you know is currently at risk. This activity will help you sort through the multiple factors associated with suicide. The activity will also help you see how to weigh these factors and assess the risk of a combination of factors like those you might see in a real person. As you complete the activity, recall that correlation does not equal causation. Even though the factors highlighted in the activity are associated with suicide, none of them necessarily cause one to attempt suicide. Nor is it the case that possessing one of these characteristics—or even several of them—means that someone *will* attempt suicide.

TIPS

- As you read the four profiles, be aware of which bits of information are or are not relevant to the likelihood of committing suicide. Once you have decided which factors are relevant, decide which ones make the subject more or less susceptible to a suicide attempt.

- If you find it difficult to sort through the profiles, take notes on a piece of paper. Make two columns for each profile: one for factors associated with an increased risk for suicide and another for factors associated with a decreased risk for suicide.

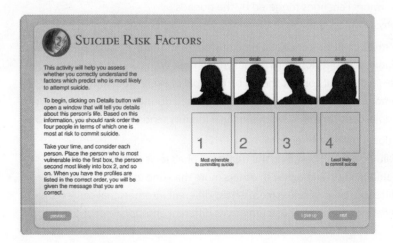

REFLECTION QUESTION

As the new high school counselor, you are in charge of creating a suicide-prevention booklet. You want to educate adolescents on detecting at-risk students. To do so, you need to create two profiles of high-risk teens. Try to create two very different profiles that have about the same level of risk.

MULTIPLE-CHOICE ITEMS

1. _____ are more likely to attempt suicide; _____ are more likely to succeed in killing themselves.
   a. Boys; boys
   b. Boys; girls
   c. Girls; boys
   d. Girls; girls

2. Of the following ethnicities—Caucasian, African American, Asian—adolescents of which group are most likely to commit suicide?
   a. Caucasian
   b. African American
   c. Asian
   d. All three are equally disposed to suicide in adolescence.

3. In the past twenty years,
   a. the suicide rates of adolescents have remained relatively stable.
   b. the suicide rates of adolescents have dramatically increased.
   c. the suicide rates of adolescents have dramatically decreased.
   d. the suicide rates of adolescents have shifted in ways similar to other age groups.

4. The personality factor associated with increased suicide susceptibility in adolescents is
   a. conscientiousness.
   b. neuroticism.
   c. extroversion.
   d. perfectionism.

5. Which of the following factors is associated with increased risk for suicide in adolescents?
   a. drug and alcohol problems
   b. feelings of depression
   c. school and family problems
   d. All of the above

CHAPTER TWELVE

Personality

12.1 Defense Mechanisms

According to Freud, people move through life blissfully unaware of the motivations for their actions. A student *thinks* he argued with his roommate because his feelings were taken for granted, when in reality the argument stemmed from his poor performance on a biology exam or from some subconscious conflict arising from early childhood. Freud believed that our subconscious camouflages the motivations for our behaviors to help us overcome the anxiety that confronting our motivations would cause. However, the long-term consequences of failing to deal with the motivations for our behavior can have serious psychological consequences: mental illness. As an analogy, consider parking in a shopping mall: most people park close to the entrance, because it is more convenient, even though the exercise of walking from far away might be more beneficial to their long-term health.

Freud identified a variety of measures that the subconscious uses to shield us from the anxiety we might feel if we understood our true motivations. He called these measures *defense mechanisms*. This activity will illustrate some of the more common defense mechanisms. Some of these mechanisms will already be familiar to you, as they have worked their way into the popular culture (e.g., repression, denial).

TIPS

- Although the illustrations of the eight defense mechanisms are good, their definitions might be hard to grasp based solely on the video. Therefore, read a written definition of each of the defense mechanisms prior to watching the videos. Definitions can be found either in your textbook or online (e.g., Wikipedia).

- Before starting the matching part of the activity on your computer, try to do it on paper first. The computer will tell you immediately if you have made an error, so working things through on paper first might give you a better sense of your level of understanding. Write down the names of the eight defense mechanisms on a piece of paper. Beneath each mechanism, write a brief description of the scenario that corresponds to that defense mechanism. Once you have matched all eight defense mechanisms, check your work using the computer.

These photos illustrate people using one of the Freudian defense mechanisms. Click on the photos to hear descriptions of the defense mechanisms. After listening to all of the descriptions, you will have a chance to assess your understanding of each one and the differences among them.

REFLECTION QUESTION

Rationalization is one of the more commonly used defense mechanisms. We often come up with logical—but untrue—reasons to explain our behaviors when the real reasons are anxiety provoking. For example, a man might claim he was fired because his boss didn't like him rather than because his performance was poor. Can you think of a time when you used such rationalization to explain your behavior? Describe the situation, and provide the real reason and the rationalization for the behavior. Did the rationalization help you feel less anxious about the situation, as Freud hypothesized?

MULTIPLE-CHOICE ITEMS

1. Which of the following is (are) true about defense mechanisms?
   a. They can distort reality.
   b. They can help us adapt to societal expectations.
   c. They can reduce anxiety.
   d. All of the above

2. After Stan's professor informed him of his failing test score, Stan banged his fists on her desk, stomped his feet on the ground, and whined that she was being unfair. Stan was coping with his anxiety by using
   a. regression.　　　　　c. projection.
   b. repression.　　　　　d. denial.

3. A man unsure of his sexuality openly discriminates against homosexuals in his workplace. The man is using _____ to deal with his inner conflict.
   a. reaction formation　　　c. sublimation
   b. displacement　　　　　d. rationalization

4. When Joan was fired from her job, she came home and yelled at her husband for forgetting to shut the refrigerator. Joan is _____ her anger toward her boss onto her husband.

   a. repressing
   b. projecting
   c. displacing
   d. rationalizing

5. After finding several receipts for hotel rooms and flowers and expensive gifts that she never received, Sharon is still convinced that her husband is not having an affair. Sharon is using which defense mechanism to minimize her anxiety?

   a. displacement
   b. regression
   c. denial
   d. sublimation

12.2 Your Ideal Self

Humanistic psychology suggests that life is a personal journey toward *self-actualization.* Self-actualization refers to a state in which a person has become exactly the kind of person that he or she wants to be. As you can imagine, self-actualization is difficult to define and therefore difficult to achieve. Self-actualization also can be fluid. Things that a young adult might consider ideal (e.g., high sociability) can lose their importance and be replaced by other characteristics (e.g., good parenting). In any case, no matter how happy and well adjusted a person might be, there is usually going to be some aspect of personality that he or she might consider "working on." The current activity will help you develop a sense of how the person you are stacks up against the person you would ideally like to be.

TIPS

- Read through all of the personality traits before you start placing them in the boxes. This will save you time from having to go back and change placements later.

- The outcome of this quick measure should not be cause for either alarm or joy. A high correlation does not indicate psychological health, nor does a low correlation indicate psychological distress. Still, it might be interesting for you to see where there are—or are not—large discrepancies between who you are and who you want to be.

Insightful	Open minded	Exercise regularly	Studious	Independent
High personal standards	Careful about appearance	Wide interest	Happy	Assertive
Responsible	Competent	Goal oriented	Eat right	Organized
A leader	Confident	Tolerant of others	Even-tempered	Adventurous
Enjoy leisure time	Helpful	Sociable	Creative	Energetic

Most Characteristic   Very Characteristic   Moderately Characteristic   Mildly Characteristic   Neutral

Most Uncharacteristic   Very Uncharacteristic   Moderately Uncharacteristic   Mildly Uncharacteristic

REFLECTION QUESTION

In this exercise you compared your actual self to your ideal self. Another comparison can be made between the "ought self" (whom I think *others* wish I would become) and the actual self. List the traits of your ought self. Is that self based on your parents' desires for you? your friends' wishes for you? someone else's hopes for you? Are these traits very similar or dissimilar to your actual self? Discrepancies between the ought self and the actual self can lead to feelings of guilt. Was this true for you?

MULTIPLE-CHOICE ITEMS

1. A state of self-fulfillment in which a person reaches his highest potential is called
   a. reaching the glass ceiling.
   b. self-regulation.
   c. self-actualization.
   d. the excellence factor.

2. The _____ is who you are. The _____ is who you would like to become.
   a. actual self; ideal self
   b. ought self; ideal self
   c. actual self; ought self
   d. ideal self; actual self

3. Discrepancies between the actual self and the ideal self
   a. rarely occur in contemporary society.
   b. can lead to high levels of anxiety.
   c. are always reduced as we age.
   d. fluctuate dramatically over the course of a day.

4. Unconditional positive regard is
   a. understanding another person from his or her own point of view.
   b. restating another person's feelings using your own words.
   c. body language that signifies caring and compassion.
   d. loving and respecting another person regardless of his or her thoughts or actions.

5. One problem with the humanistic approach is that
   a. it relies too heavily on the unconscious mind.
   b. it offers no hope for the human condition.
   c. it places too much emphasis on rewards and punishments.
   d. the assumption that people are basically good is unverifiable.

12.3 Trait Theory of Personality

Think about one of your close friends. Why do you like this person so much? Now think about someone whom you don't particularly like, not someone who has wronged you in some way but someone who just kind of rubs you the wrong way. What is it about this person that causes you to have these feelings? The simple answer to both questions usually relates to something we might informally call *personality*. Some people's personalities just suit us better than others. Psychologists have worked for decades to develop a better sense of the components of personality; that is, what are the basic building blocks that make you who you are? One influential school of thought is trait theory. Traits are personality characteristics that are relatively stable: they do not change much as people grow older, nor do they change much based on the situation. According to trait theory, a person who is friendly will be just as friendly twenty years from now as he or she is today. The person will also be friendly whether dealing with someone new or someone he or she knows very well. There is some variability in traits based on the situation—even a friendly person may be brusque if in a hurry—but a friendly person will tend to be more friendly than other people in the same situation.

There are at least two problems associated with trait theories of personality. First, not everyone believes that traits are the best way to measure personality. Second, even those who believe that traits are the best measure of personality do not necessarily agree on which traits are most central to personality. This activity will introduce you to one particular trait theory that many researchers subscribe to: the Big Five. You will learn the five components of this theory and have an opportunity to learn how each of these components contributes to personality and, ultimately, influences behavior.

- After you have selected the right candidate to be manager of the Café Cogito, go back and select a less well-qualified candidate, and try to predict how this candidate will fail.

- Once you understand the Big Five traits, see whether your close friends tend to share common traits. Do your friends tend to be extraverted? conscientious? open to new experiences? What about people you are less inclined to be friends with? Do they share traits in common? Are those traits different from the traits of your close friends?

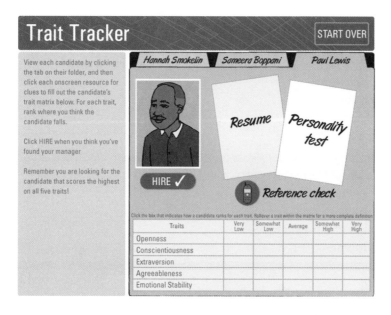

REFLECTION QUESTION

Although trait theorists agree that five traits lie at the core of a person's personality, they point out that individuals vary greatly in the degree and quantity to which a particular trait applies. Consider your own personality. Where do you think you fall (high versus low) on each of the Big Five traits? Was it easier to place yourself on some dimensions than on others? Do you think your personality is fully explained using only these five dimensions?

MULTIPLE-CHOICE ITEMS

1. Which of the following is *not* a Big Five personality factor?
   a. conscientiousness
   b. agreeableness
   c. perfectionism
   d. extraversion

2. Andrew is quite talkative and fun loving. He loves to socialize with others and enjoys being around other people. Andrew would score high on which personality factor?
   a. agreeableness
   b. extraversion
   c. conscientiousness
   d. openness to experience

3. George is a worrier. He always seems tense, because he is anxious about his health, his job, and his relationships. Which factor of personality best encapsulates these attributes of George?
   a. extraversion
   b. neuroticism
   c. conscientiousness
   d. agreeableness

4. A person high in _____ might try skydiving or bungee jumping.
   a. agreeableness
   b. neuroticism
   c. extraversion
   d. openness to experience

5. When selecting a partner for a class project that is to determine 50 percent of your grade, you would be best served picking a person high in
   a. conscientiousness.
   b. extraversion.
   c. openness to experience.
   d. neuroticism.

12.4 Personality Assessment

As you have read, there are many theories of personality. Each of these theories identifies certain personal traits or characteristics as being the keys to understanding personality. Of course, it is not sufficient for a theory to identify the basic building blocks of personality. The theory must also provide a way of measuring or assessing these aspects of personality. As the text portion of this activity indicates, psychologists have developed three classes of personality test: self-report measures, projective tests, and behavioral measurements. Each of these kinds of tests has strengths and drawbacks. Behavioral measurements allow the psychologist an extended window of observation into the behavior of the test subject, although they can be time consuming and require special training to assess. Projective tests are easier to administer, but they are subject to interpretation, and different psychologists might read the results of the same set of responses differently. Self-report tests are easy to administer and to interpret, but people might not answer these tests honestly, especially if the test is designed to measure some negative characteristic. This activity will allow you to participate in a self-report measure of personality so you can see the strengths and weaknesses of this kind of personality assessment.

TIPS

- Do not respond too quickly to the questions on the personality assessment. Thinking carefully about your responses will provide the best opportunity for the test to return an accurate assessment of your personality.

- After completing the activity, go back and retake the test, changing your responses to see how the different set of responses changes your personality profile.

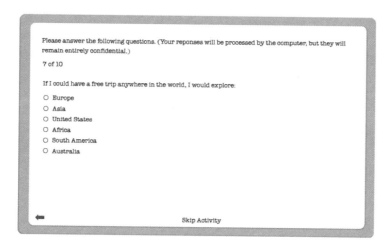

Please answer the following questions. (Your reponses will be processed by the computer, but they will remain entirely confidential.)

7 of 10

If I could have a free trip anywhere in the world, I would explore:

○ Europe
○ Asia
○ United States
○ Africa
○ South America
○ Australia

Skip Activity

REFLECTION QUESTION

Have you ever had your handwriting analyzed? Do you believe your astrological profile is accurate? People often believe that these methods of personality assessment are quite accurate, even though the profiles are often made up. Why are people so willing to believe false information regarding their personalities? Specifically, what factors contribute to our tendency to believe these profiles?

MULTIPLE-CHOICE ITEMS

1. Chase is shown an ambiguous picture and asked to interpret it. Chase is most likely taking a(n) _____ personality test.
   a. self-report
   b. projective
   c. behavioral assessment
   d. objective

2. Bailey answers a series of questions about herself, ranging from her birth order to her attitudes about socializing. Which type of personality-assessment method has Bailey completed?
   a. projective
   b. behavioral assessment
   c. self-report
   d. implicit association

3. Which of the following is true of students' beliefs regarding their Stewart Personality Inventory profiles?
   a. Students believed the information was very accurate.
   b. Students believed the information was lacking insight.
   c. Students believed the information was not personalized.
   d. Students believed the information was bogus.

4. One of the dangers of self-report personality measures is that
   a. a person's behavior may change dramatically from one test session to the next.
   b. the unconscious is impossible to measure.
   c. the test administrator often projects his biases onto the test responses.
   d. people tend to believe the results even though they may have no validity.

5. One factor that contributes to a person's tendency to believe a false personality profile is that
   a. the profiles are generally negative.
   b. the profiles are very specific.
   c. the profiles lack information.
   d. the profiles are very sophisticated.

Health Psychology

13.1 College Stress Test

Finals week: a caffeine-fueled, five-to-seven-day sleepless obstacle course. And what is the reward at the end of the week? Well, if you are like many other college students, the answer will be a cold with flulike symptoms. After a week of poor eating and sleeping habits, your body becomes too tired to fight off whatever virus might be circulating around campus. This scenario illustrates the way stress can affect our bodies. It can help us face and overcome challenges like finals week, but it can also wear our bodies down and make us more susceptible to both physical illnesses and emotional distress. People are able to cope with stress to differing degrees and employ different strategies to help get themselves "over the hump." Thus, it is difficult to tell how much stress someone is undergoing simply by observing her or his behavior. Fortunately, objective measures of life stressors have been developed that take into account not only how many stressful events someone is facing but the severity of those events as well. This activity will allow you to complete a stress test geared toward college-aged individuals—similar tests have been developed for people in other age ranges—so that you can obtain a sense of how truly stressed you are.

TIPS

- It is important to note that positive events, like starting a new relationship, can also be sources of stress.

- Remember that different individuals have different levels of tolerance for stress. Falling into the "high-stress" category may not be unhealthful for some people, whereas others who fall within the "normal" range may feel overwhelmed. If you are feeling overwhelmed, you should seek help, regardless of how you scored on the test.

- Speaking of seeking help, be sure to read the information at the end of the activity carefully, as it provides useful tips for dealing with stress. Even if you are not feeling terribly stressed today, it could help you later in the semester (during finals?) or later in life.

Please indicate whether you have experienced any of the following events in the past year by clicking "yes" or "no."

yes	no	
○	○	Being raped
○	○	Finding out that you are HIV-Positive
○	○	Being accused of rape
○	○	Death of a close friend
○	○	Death of a close family member
○	○	Contracting a sexually transmitted disease (other than AIDS)
○	○	Concerns about being pregnant
○	○	Finals week
○	○	Concerns about your partner being pregnant
○	○	Oversleeping for an exam
○	○	Flunking a class
○	○	Having a boyfriend or girlfriend cheat on you
○	○	Ending a steady dating relationship

1/4

SKIP ACTIVITY

REFLECTION QUESTIONS

1. According to the College Stress Test, how stressed are you? Did you fall into the normal range, or are you overstressed? Do you think the test is valid? That is, do you think it accurately measures stress levels in college students? Why or why not? Were you surprised by the inclusion of any of the items because you don't view them as stressful? Why?

2. Events that give us pleasure can also cause considerable stress. Select an event from the list in the activity that has brought you both pleasure and stress in the past year. What made the event pleasurable? What made the event stressful? Did the pleasure outweigh the stress or vice versa? Did you do anything to try to reduce the stress during the event?

MULTIPLE-CHOICE ITEMS

1. The average college student experiences approximately _____ stressful events every year.
   a. 5 to 10
   b. 15 to 20
   c. 25 to 30
   d. 35 to 40

2. According to the College Stress Test, which of the following events is considered the *least* stressful?
   a. commuting to campus
   b. talking in front of a class
   c. finding out you are HIV positive
   d. cheating on your significant other

3. Research on stress in college students has found that
   a. some students never experience a stressful event.
   b. common events such as attending an athletic event typically do not cause a person stress.
   c. all individuals tend to react to stressful events in the same way.
   d. even normal events, such as registering for classes, can cause stress.

4. On the same day that Tyler had two important exams, he found out that his girlfriend had been cheating on him. Cecila, a freshman, is living away from home and trying to maintain a 4.0 grade-point average. Based on this information, who would have a higher stress score?
   a. Tyler
   b. Cecila
   c. Tyler and Cecila would have similar scores.
   d. It is impossible to determine.

5. Which of the following is *not* a suggestion for relieving stress?
   a. exercise
   b. eating well
   c. drinking alcoholic beverages
   d. meditation

13.2 Type A Behavior

The desire to accomplish goals is generally a positive personal attribute, but like anything else, too much of a good thing can be destructive. A pair of cardiologists noticed that many of the heart attack victims they treated had tended to share a common personality profile that combined an obsessive need to compete with an excessive need to win. They labeled this profile the *type A personality.* As you know, correlation does not prove causation, so the fact that heart disease tended to occur frequently in type A men did not prove that having a particular personality type made it more likely that such a person would suffer a heart attack. However, several subsequent lines of evidence are consistent with the view that the type A personality leads to cardiac problems. For example, healthy men were tracked over the course of several years. Those with type A personalities were more likely to suffer a subsequent heart attack. As well, men who suffered a heart attack and then changed their lifestyles to allow for more relaxation and lower needs for competition and conquest were less likely to suffer additional heart problems than those who did not alter their lifestyles. This activity will allow you to learn more about the components of the type A personality and will also enable you to assess the extent to which you conform to this personality type.

- Remember that even if a strong causal link between having a type A personality and cardiovascular disease were a 100-percent certainty, these kinds of relationships could not predict individual cases. In other words, scoring high on this measure of type A personality traits does not mean that you are destined to suffer a heart attack. However, if you are concerned or unhappy about your scores, you might want to reflect on how you could alter some of your behaviors.

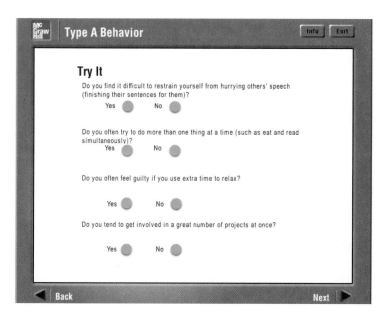

REFLECTION QUESTIONS

1. Think of a friend or family member whom you would definitely label type A. Now think of a friend or family member whom you would definitely label type B. Imagine that you are going to see a movie with these two people. Even though you arrive at the movie fifteen minutes before it starts, the lines are incredibly long and it is clear you will be late for the movie. Describe how each of your companions will react in this situation.

2. Now imagine that you are at home with both of these people and one other person. It is game night! You are going to form pairs and play a series of games, and the overall losing pair must buy the winning pair dinner. Based on what you have learned about type A behavior, do you want to have the type A or type B person as your teammate? Explain.

1. Most people can be categorized as
    a. type A.
    b. type B.
    c. in between type A and type B.
    d. in between type B and type C.

2. John is always on the go, trying to accomplish as much as he can in as little time as possible. He does not like waiting in traffic and gets rather angry when he is delayed. It seems he just cannot relax in these situations. John exhibits
    a. type A behavior.
    b. type B behavior.
    c. behavior that falls between type A and type B.
    d. behavior that is neither type A nor type B.

3. John's younger brother, Scott, is definitely a type B personality. Which of the following behaviors is Scott likely to exhibit?
    a. becoming impatient while waiting for his order at a restaurant
    b. getting angry when he loses a competition
    c. honking at a stalled car in front of him
    d. relaxing in front of a roaring fire

4. Research on the link between type A behavior and heart disease found that
    a. men with type A behavior showed a decreased likelihood of developing heart disease in late life.
    b. men with type A behavior showed an increased likelihood of developing heart disease in late life.
    c. type A behavior causes heart disease.
    d. the link between type A behavior and heart disease has decreased over the last five decades.

5. Which of the following is *false* regarding type A behavior?
    a. People with type A behavior are often successful.
    b. People with type A behavior can easily change to a different behavioral style.
    c. Type A features can be altered with relaxation training or assertiveness training.
    d. People with type A behavior often show unusual amounts of hostility.

CHAPTER FOURTEEN

Abnormal Psychology:
Therapy and Treatment

14.1 Distinguishing Abnormality: A Continuum View

One of the most difficult jobs for a psychologist is to decide whether someone's behavior can be considered abnormal. There are a wide range of behaviors that people engage in, and things that may seem perfectly natural to you might be considered either strange or maladaptive to someone else. For example, would you parachute out of an airplane thousands of feet off the ground? Some people might consider this behavior much too risky to consider. Would you consider getting a body piercing or tattooing a large portion of your body? How would you evaluate someone who got a piercing or tattoo? By comparison, how would your parents (who presumably grew up in a time when body piercing and tattooing were less common) evaluate such a person? Fortunately, psychologists have a set of criteria to evaluate whether a particular behavior is adaptive, unhealthful, or neutral. This activity will introduce you to the four major criteria that psychologists use to evaluate abnormality: "physically damaging," "lost touch with reality," "emotional suffering," and "interferes with ability to function." This activity will also give you a chance to categorize the behaviors of some virtual characters.

TIPS

- Study the four criteria so that you will remember them throughout the activity. You can write them down if you wish, but committing them to memory now may help you remember them later in the semester when you might encounter these terms on a quiz or exam.

- The criteria presented here are very general and apply to the full spectrum of psychiatric disorders. Diagnosing a specific disorder requires consultation with the *Diagnostic and Statistical Manual* (see Activity 14.2, "Understanding the *DSM*").

- As the name of this activity implies, abnormality exists on a continuum. Many people exhibit some behaviors that might fall into one of the four categories listed above at one time or another. The fact that you can reflect on some behaviors in the past that might be abnormal is not necessarily cause for alarm, but if reflecting on your own behavior makes you anxious, you might consider speaking with a member of the counseling center at your school.

REFLECTION QUESTION

Our perception of the physical world is influenced by our expectations. This general rule of perception extends to people as well. Our evaluations are colored by our past experiences with people or by other cues like the way they dress. How do you think you would have evaluated the behavior of the characters in this activity if you had initially been told which one of them had been diagnosed with a mental disorder?

MULTIPLE-CHOICE ITEMS

1. Your roommate becomes depressed after he learns that his significant other has been cheating on him. He skips class for the next week. His behavior would fall under which category of abnormal behavior?
   a. physically damaging
   b. lost touch with reality
   c. interferes with ability to function
   d. All of the above

2. For several days, Joe has been crying periodically and has had difficulty sleeping and eating. His behavior
   a. would definitely be considered normal.
   b. would definitely be considered abnormal.
   c. would be difficult to categorize as normal or abnormal without knowing the cause of his behavior.
   d. is not relevant to a judgment of normality/abnormality.

3. A schizophrenic patient refuses to leave his home because he claims that the government is monitoring his thoughts using tiny microwave transmitters hidden inside traffic signals. This behavior would be considered evidence of

   a. loss of touch with reality.

   b. interference with the ability to function.

   c. Neither a nor b

   d. Both a and b

4. Clare has entered the manic phase of bipolar disorder. She has trouble sleeping and has gotten herself into financial trouble by buying a car that she cannot really afford. Despite these problems, Clare feels as though she is on top of the world. Clare's behavior would be considered evidence of

   a. emotional suffering.

   b. loss of touch with reality.

   c. a physically damaging action.

   d. None of the above

14.2 Understanding the *DSM*

When doctors are confronted by patients with unfamiliar sets of symptoms, they consult a large reference book called the *Physicians' Desk Reference,* which lists the symptoms and treatment options for every known disease. When psychologists are confronted by a patient with an unfamiliar set of symptoms, they consult a large reference book called the *DSM-IV-TR. DSM* stands for *Diagnostic and Statistical Manual.* The *DSM* has been through several major and minor revisions; thus, the roman numeral IV and the *TR* that follow the letters *DSM* refer to the most recently updated version of the *DSM.* The *DSM* helps ensure that psychologists in different clinics and with different kinds of backgrounds use the same criteria both for diagnosing disorders and formulating treatment options. Standardizing the way patients are diagnosed and treated helps ensure that both current and future generations of patients are given the best possible psychological care.

This activity will illustrate the way the *DSM-IV-TR* is organized and will give you an opportunity to experience how this reference is used to help recognize the symptoms of different disorders, both from verbal descriptions and by observing the behavior of individuals.

T I P

- Watch the videos that describe the different axes of mental disorders carefully. You might jot down a few notes while you are listening, as you will be asked about the kinds of symptoms associated with the disorders illustrated in the videos.

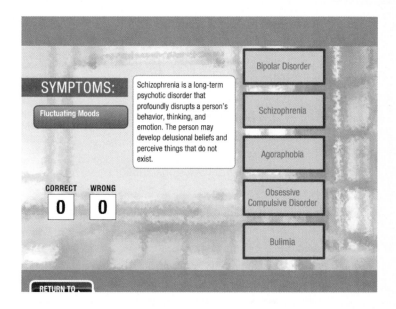

SYMPTOMS:

Fluctuating Moods

Schizophrenia is a long-term psychotic disorder that profoundly disrupts a person's behavior, thinking, and emotion. The person may develop delusional beliefs and perceive things that do not exist.

CORRECT   WRONG
   0   0

Bipolar Disorder

Schizophrenia

Agoraphobia

Obsessive Compulsive Disorder

Bulimia

RETURN TO

REFLECTION QUESTION

Imagine you work for your university's mental health clinic. Carlotta comes to your office and tells you that she has been feeling depressed and can not seem to concentrate on her studies. How would you fully assess Carlotta's mental health by using each of the 5 Axes as discussed in the video? That is, what sorts of questions would each of the 5 axes address? For example, how might different responses to questions posed by Axis III lead you to reach a different conclusion regarding Carlotta's health? What might Carlotta's responses to Axis IV questions reveal?

MULTIPLE CHOICE ITEMS

1. Disorders such as Major Depression, Schizophrenia, and Bulimia Nervosa are classified as _____disorders.
   a. Axis I
   b. Axis II
   c. Axis III
   d. Axis IV

2. Personality disorders are different from Axis I disorders in which way(s)?
   a. They tend to persist for long periods of time, often lasting a lifetime.
   b. They are difficult to treat.
   c. Both a and b
   d. Neither a nor b

3. Axis III information would help a psychologist to
   a. Determine if Susan had a personality disorder or a psychotic disorder.
   b. Determine if Bill's recent depressive state was preceded by a recent divorce.
   c. Determine if Elizabeth's panic attacks were sparked by memories of her deceased father.
   d. Determine if Tom's hallucinations were associated with a brain tumor.

4. Axis V assessment directly examines a person's
   a. Overall level of functioning.
   b. Propensity to lie about symptoms.
   c. Ability to distinguish reality from delusional thought
   d. General physical health.

5. The *DSM-IV* can be used for diagnosing psychological disorders:
   a. By anyone who has completed a relevant course in psychology.
   b. By anyone who purchases the book and carefully reads its entire contents.
   c. By qualified mental health professionals who have had extensive education and training.
   d. By individuals who have completed a medical degree.

14.3 Depression

Many people have experienced depression either firsthand or by observing someone close to them. As a result, many people think that they know depression, when in fact it is much more complex than most people realize. As the video will describe, there are a variety of factors that may make one susceptible to depression, including genetic/biological factors and stressful life events. Depression is also associated with many symptoms beyond feeling down or sad, including disruptions in sleeping or eating patterns and lack of motivation. Finally, a number of treatment plans are available to those suffering from depression. This video describes one particular biochemical treatment that has become very popular: selective serotonin reuptake inhibitors, often called SSRIs. Even if you are not familiar with this psychiatric term, you may find that you are familiar with the names of some of the common SSRIs discussed in the video.

TIPS

- Bear in mind that antidepression medications are not the magical cure that they may appear to be in this video. You may wish to do a little online investigation to learn more about some of the concerns surrounding this class of drug and the possibility that, as the video mentions, it is being overprescribed.

- It is also useful to note that an antidepression medication is often combined with other forms of treatment, including regular counseling. This combined approach is designed to address the multiple "causes" of depression cited above.

 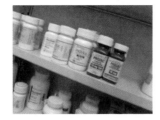 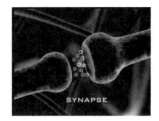

REFLECTION QUESTION

The video alludes to the fact that some professionals are concerned that Prozac and other antidepression medications may be overprescribed. The concern is not because these drugs cause side effects. What are some other reasons why a psychologist or psychiatrist might be concerned about the overprescription of these drugs? Hint: think about how genes and the environment influence one's susceptibility to depression.

MULTIPLE-CHOICE ITEMS

1. Which of the following is a known cause of depression?
   a. family history
   b. neurochemical imbalances
   c. negative life events
   d. All of the above

2. Research on the causes of depression suggests that
   a. environmental factors are usually more important than genetic factors.
   b. genetic factors are usually more important than environmental factors.
   c. genetic and environmental factors are equally important, but in any particular case, one is generally primarily responsible.
   d. genetic and environmental factors usually combine to produce depression.

3. Relative to nondepressed people, depressed people generally have
   a. less serotonin.
   b. more serotonin.
   c. less acetylcholine.
   d. more acetylcholine.

4. Prozac and similar drugs alleviate depression by
   a. increasing the amount of neurotransmitter in the synapse.
   b. decreasing the amount of neurotransmitter in the synapse.
   c. increasing the number of synapses in the brain.
   d. decreasing the number of synapses in the brain.

5. Drugs treat depression by
   a. making the patient happy.
   b. distracting the patient from negative events in his or her life.
   c. helping the patient regulate his or her mood.
   d. helping the patient focus during therapy.

14.4 Bipolar Disorder

Most people are familiar with the term *depression* and its associated symptoms: negative thoughts and feelings, hopelessness, and lack of energy and motivation. However, in some individuals, feelings of depression alternate with feelings of mania. Manic episodes are associated with heightened excitability, energy, euphoria, and invincibility. As you can see, the symptoms for manic episodes are the polar opposite of those experienced during depression. Therefore, people who suffer from cycles of depression followed by mania followed by depression are said to be suffering from *bipolar disorder* (nonpsychologists often refer to this disorder as *manic depression*). In this activity, a subject known as Bernie will describe some of his experiences of manic depression. As you will see, although the symptoms associated with mania may seem positive, they are often associated with serious costs.

TIPS

- People who care for loved ones with bipolar disorder often report that the manic episodes are more difficult to deal with than the depressed episodes. As you listen to Bernie, try to figure out why this is so.

- People suffering from bipolar disorder have a terrible track record of taking medication to control the manic episodes. As you listen to Bernie speak, try to figure out why this is so.

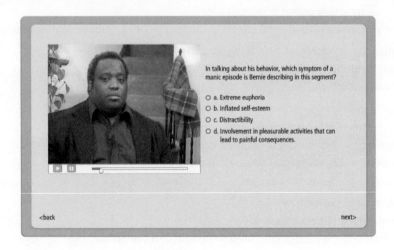

In talking about his behavior, which symptom of a manic episode is Bernie describing in this segment?

○ a. Extreme euphoria
○ b. Inflated self-esteem
○ c. Distractibility
○ d. Involvement in pleasurable activities that can lead to painful consequences.

<back   next>

REFLECTION QUESTIONS

1. Have you ever known someone with bipolar disorder? An episode of mania is characterized by several key symptoms. A person might not demonstrate all of these symptoms during a manic episode, but she or he often displays many of them. Based on what you have learned in this exercise, create a short description of "Fred," who is experiencing a manic episode. Try to exemplify as many of the symptoms as you can in describing Fred.

2. Many people with bipolar disorder relish their manic episodes. Why do you think this is? What are some positive outcomes that could be associated with mania? That is, how might a manic episode be useful to a person? On the other hand, how might a manic episode be quite troublesome and problematic?

MULTIPLE-CHOICE ITEMS

1. Bipolar disorder is classified as a(n)
   a. psychotic disorder.
   b. dissociative disorder.
   c. mood disorder.
   d. anxiety disorder.

2. Which of the following is *not* a symptom of bipolar disorder?
   a. manic episode
   b. depressive episode
   c. unwarranted fears
   d. significant impairment in everyday living

3. Bipolar disorder typically involves periods of both
   a. obsessions and compulsions.
   b. bingeing and purging.
   c. delusions and hallucinations.
   d. mania and depression.

4. In the last few days, Ginger has felt very euphoric and energetic. She does not seem to need much sleep and is able to get large amounts of work done during the night hours. She feels as if she can do it all. Ginger is probably experiencing a(n)
   a. manic episode.
   b. depressive episode.
   c. obsessive episode.
   d. compulsive episode.

5. People in a depressive episode often
   a. have inflated self-esteem.
   b. show increased activity.
   c. experience high levels of fatigue.
   d. engage in overly promiscuous behavior.

14.5 Phobia

Everyone experiences fears from time to time. There is nothing abnormal about the anxiety one feels while preparing to bungee jump. Standing on top of a rickety old bridge strapped to a few rubber bands should elicit some concerns about the possibility of dying. *Phobias,* however, are fears that are abnormal in at least two ways. First, the anxiety felt by the phobic individual is out of proportion to the danger posed by the fear-inducing stimulus. Second, the anxiety interferes with the completion of common daily activities. Spiders are a good example for distinguishing between a fear and a phobia. Many people find spiders icky and would prefer not to have one crawling on them. A fear of spiders might also give us pause before entering a dusty attic or a dark cave where they are likely to be. Either of these behaviors might be considered evidence of a fear of spiders. However, an aversion to spiders would not be considered a phobia unless a person felt that the spiders posed a real physical danger, which is rarely the case in the Western Hemisphere. A phobia would also produce an aversion to entering rooms that most people would expect to be free of spiders and might cause the phobic person to engage in elaborate cleaning rituals before entering a space that might contain spiders. These elaborate rituals interfere with the person's carrying out normal activities in a timely fashion. This activity will introduce you to Annie, a woman suffering from an often misunderstood kind of phobia: agoraphobia.

TIPS

- As you will see, the common belief that agoraphobia is a fear of open spaces is a myth. As you listen to Annie, try to understand the true nature of agoraphobia, but also think about why this misunderstanding about agoraphobia continues to persist.

- If you are like most people, you probably suffer at least a moderate fear of public speaking. On the surface, this might seem to have much in common with agoraphobia. But as you listen to Annie, think about why agoraphobia is a phobia, whereas fear of public speaking is not.

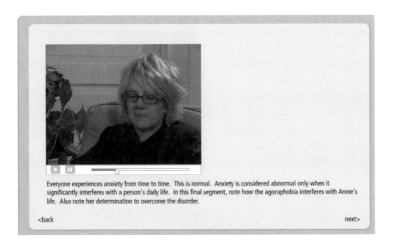

Everyone experiences anxiety from time to time. This is normal. Anxiety is considered abnormal only when it significantly interferes with a person's daily life. In this final segment, note how the agoraphobia interferes with Annie's life. Also note her determination to overcome the disorder.

<back   next>

REFLECTION QUESTION

Although agoraphobia is a relatively rare disorder, we all experience fears from time to time. Sometimes our fears have very clear beginnings. For example, a person who experiences a very turbulent flight might develop a fear of flying. At other times, however, we are unaware of why our fears exist. What is something that you fear? It can be an object, a situation, a behavior, or an outcome. Do you know why you have this fear? Can you pinpoint its origins? How anxious are you when presented with the fear-inducing stimuli? What do you do to reduce anxiety in these situations?

MULTIPLE-CHOICE ITEMS

1. Agoraphobia is a(n)
   a. anxiety disorder.
   b. mood disorder.
   c. dissociative disorder.
   d. psychotic disorder.

2. Janis has been diagnosed with agoraphobia. She most likely
   a. fears a very specific object such as a snake or a needle.
   b. fears she will experience an anxiety attack in a public setting where escape or assistance is not available.
   c. fears that bad things will happen to her if she does not engage in specific repetitive behaviors.
   d. fears large open spaces.

3. _____ percent of the population will suffer from agoraphobia at one time or another.
   a. One
   b. Three
   c. Five
   d. Ten

4. As he is walking to his car in a busy parking lot, Don's heart starts racing. He begins to sweat profusely and has difficulty breathing. He feels dizzy and believes he might pass out. Don is probably experiencing a
   a. compulsion.
   b. manic episode.
   c. panic attack.
   d. dissociation.

5. Anxiety is considered abnormal
   a. when it significantly interferes with a person's daily life.
   b. when it is experienced mildly several times a week.
   c. whenever it occurs.
   d. only when it forces a person to be hospitalized.

14.6 Schizophrenia

Many of us have heard the term *psychotic* used informally to describe someone who is behaving bizarrely or dangerously. Psychologists use this term to refer to behavior that demonstrates an inability to appreciate reality. Psychotic behavior can take many forms:

- Seeing objects or hearing voices that are not actually present
- Believing that alien beings from another planet have taken over the earth and are covertly orchestrating the actions of the government and/or individuals

Although psychotic behavior can be observed in a variety of mental disorders, *schizophrenia* is one of the most commonly observed and most debilitating psychotic diseases. People who suffer from schizophrenia often wind up living on the margins of society because their inability to respond normally makes it difficult for them to hold a job and take care of routine activities like cooking, cleaning, and paying rent.

Schizophrenia also takes many different forms, which do not necessarily resemble one another. This makes diagnosis more difficult. Finally, the inability to maintain a coherent sense of reality makes it difficult for schizophrenic individuals to follow medical treatments unless they are closely supervised. As such, many wind up confined to psychiatric-care facilities with 24-hour supervision. Obviously, the expense associated with these facilities is another reason why schizophrenic individuals end up living on the margins. The present activity includes interviews with two people diagnosed with schizophrenia to give you a better perspective of how behavior is affected by this disease.

TIPS

- As mentioned, there are several different kinds of schizophrenia. As you watch the videos, note as many differences as possible between the subjects. This will help you later when you learn how to distinguish between the various subtypes of schizophrenia.

- Nonpsychologists often confuse schizophrenia with dissociative identity disorder, in which an individual manifests several distinct personalities. As you watch the videos, think about why this common misconception might exist.

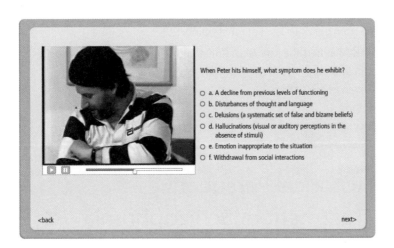

REFLECTION QUESTION

You viewed video clips of Valerie and Peter, two individuals diagnosed with schizophrenia. Although both people have the same diagnosis, their symptoms are quite different. Briefly describe the symptoms that each person demonstrated. Despite their different presentations, how are Peter and Valerie similarly affected by this disorder?

MULTIPLE-CHOICE ITEMS

1. The symptoms of schizophrenia
   a. can vary dramatically over time.
   b. do not manifest until a person is in his or her late 30s or 40s.
   c. do not impair the individual's sense of reality.
   d. are typically minor and often unnoticeable.

2. All of the following are symptoms of schizophrenia, *except*
   a. thought and language disturbance.
   b. emotion inappropriate to the situation.
   c. withdrawal from social interaction.
   d. long periods of sleeplessness.

3. Dana, a hospital admitting clerk, believes that the FBI is reading her e-mails at work in an effort to convict her of communicating with aliens. Dana is exhibiting which symptom of schizophrenia?
   a. hallucinations
   b. delusions
   c. language disturbances
   d. inappropriate emotions

4. Kerrick, when told about his grandfather's sudden death, began to laugh aloud. The symptom of schizophrenia that Kerrick demonstrated is
   a. emotion inappropriate to the situation.
   b. disturbances in thought and language.
   c. a hallucination.
   d. decline from previous level of functioning.

5. When Valerie claimed she saw Jesus Christ in the heavens, she was experiencing
   a. emotion inappropriate to the situation.
   b. an obsessive thought.
   c. a delusion.
   d. a hallucination.

14.7 Historical Perspectives: Treatment of Schizophrenia

Nowadays, people suffering from mental illnesses are treated with sympathy. Treatment programs are designed to maximize the possibility that mentally ill individuals can live productive, independent lives. This was not always the case. Throughout most of human history, mentally ill people were shunned, shackled, tortured, or even killed. The treatment of mental illness was primarily about protecting society from those who were sick rather than trying to help those who were suffering. Clearly, a lot of progress has been made, although there are still ways in which our treatment of the mentally ill can be improved. This video provides a quick overview of how the victims of mental illness have been treated over the years.

TIPS

- Think about how views regarding the causes of mental illness have changed over the years and how these views have influenced the treatment of mentally ill individuals.

- How do current views of the causes of mental illness influence the way mentally ill people are treated today? How do you think people will view the current treatment of mental illness 100 years from now? What role do you think psychological and medical research will play in changing attitudes toward mental illness and its treatment?

REFLECTION QUESTION

Tracing the history of the treatment of mental illness makes it clear that diseases like schizophrenia are approached more empathically than they have been at any other point in history. What do you think is responsible for the change in the way mentally ill people are treated? Is it the result of medical or scientific breakthroughs? changes in religious doctrine? a moral shift in the way we treat less fortunate members of society?

MULTIPLE-CHOICE ITEMS

1. In ancient times, mental illness was attributed to
   a. environmental causes.
   c. physical causes.
   b. psychological causes.
   d. religious causes.

2. In the Middle Ages, mental illness was attributed to
   a. environmental causes.
   c. physical causes.
   b. psychological causes.
   d. religious causes.

3. The attempt to cure mental illness by shocking or cutting it out of the body
   a. was observed in ancient times but abandoned in the Middle Ages.
   b. was observed up through the Middle Ages but abandoned early in the nineteenth century.
   c. continued well into the twentieth century.
   d. was practiced by alternative healers but not by the medical community.

4. For much of human history, mentally ill people were restricted to asylums to
   a. separate them from the rest of society.
   b. facilitate the study of mental illness.
   c. better provide for the needs of mentally ill individuals.
   d. protect them from the harsh treatment they would have received in the outside world.

5. In general, drug therapies for schizophrenia
   a. treat the symptoms of the disease but not the causes.
   b. treat the causes of the disease but not the symptoms.
   c. help to some degree but don't allow patients to live outside of mental institutions.
   d. tend to work best when combined with surgical treatments.

14.8 Substance Abuse

Drug and substance abuse is often considered to be a social or societal problem, but its greatest impact can be felt by the individuals and family members touched by alcohol or drug addictions. This video presents the story of Bobbi and her descent into drug abuse. In her own words, she describes how she began to use controlled substances—starting with cigarettes—at a very young age and progressed steadily to ever more dangerous drugs. Although shocking, her story is representative of many people whose lives have been taken over by the daily need for controlled substances. To people who have never suffered through an addiction, it may be hard to understand how the craving for a drug can overpower more reasonable instincts. One way to come to terms with the battle between addiction and reason is to think of the biological activity that produces addictive behavior. The video "The Neurochemical Basis of Addiction" will give you a sense of the powerful neural signals that make battling an addiction such an overwhelming task.

TIPS

- The beginning of Bobbi's video presents a definition of substance abuse. As you watch the video, think about how her story satisfies this definition.
- As you listen to Bobbi's story, think about the extent to which nature and nurture influenced Bobbi's behavior.

Substance abuse is another example of how biological and environmental/psychological factors combine to produce behavior. How does Bobbi's story demonstrate the combination of biological and environmental/psychological factors that produce depression? Why do drugs that stimulate pleasure centers of the brain become particularly appealing to people suffering through periods of personal problems? Why isn't everyone who suffers through a difficult period equally susceptible to substance abuse and dependence?

MULTIPLE-CHOICE ITEMS

1. Substance abuse is commonly defined as
   a. any drug use without a prescription.
   b. any drug use by an underage individual.
   c. any drug use that influences mood.
   d. any drug use that causes significant personal or legal problems and frequently places the individual in unsafe situations.

2. The fact that drugs like naltrexone can help people with alcohol dependence is consistent with the idea that alcohol dependence is at least partially caused by
   a. psychological factors.
   b. genetic factors.
   c. biological factors.
   d. All of the above

3. According to the video, neither naltrexone nor any other drug will eliminate the need for therapy. This conclusion implies that alcohol abuse is at least partially caused by
   a. psychological factors.
   b. genetic factors.
   c. biological factors.
   d. All of the above

4. It is believed that naltrexone blocks opioid receptors. As a result, naltrexone
   a. reduces the amount of alcohol needed to produce an effect.
   b. reduces the "kick" that alcohol typically provides.
   c. causes alcohol to make one physically ill.
   d. causes dehydration.

5. People continue to abuse drugs in spite of the negative consequences because
   a. drugs influence the pleasure centers of the brain.
   b. drugs have biological but not psychological effects on users.
   c. drugs have psychological but not biological effects on users.
   d. users are generally unaware of the negative consequences that drugs have on their lives.

14.9 Eating Disorders

Here are two videos about eating disorders. The first shows Dr. Graciela Andreson, a clinical psychologist, talking about the major categories of eating disorders and their associated symptoms. Note that this psychologist takes a psychodynamic approach to understanding eating disorders. That is, she argues that the primary cause of eating disorders does not concern food or weight. Instead, the patient is struggling with some deeper psychological conflict that is being expressed through disordered eating behavior.

TIPS

- As you watch the second video, think about what type of eating disorder is most similar to the behavior the woman describes. Bear in mind that accurate diagnoses of eating disorders require both extensive training and more information than is contained in this short video clip.

- Pay careful attention to what Dr. Andreson identifies as the primary psychological issue for people with eating disorders. Is this assertion supported by the testimony of the woman who describes her own experiences in the second video?

From time to time, we all eat more food in a short period of time than we probably should. However, these incidents are much different in quality and quantity from a bulimic episode. Think of a time when you overate, and describe the food you ate. Now describe the food that the woman in the second video ate. How are these descriptions different from each other? Why do you think you overate? How is your reasoning different from the reasoning of the woman in the video?

MULTIPLE-CHOICE ITEMS

1. *Bulimia nervosa* involves
   a. ingesting very large amounts of food in a short period of time.
   b. ridding oneself of large amounts of food quickly (via vomiting, laxatives, etc.).
   c. Both a and b
   d. Neither a nor b

2. Most women and girls with eating disorders are concerned with issues of
   a. control.
   b. extroversion.
   c. mood swings.
   d. intelligence.

3. Susie has *anorexia nervosa*. Her body weight is dramatically lower than what is normal for her size and age. She eats very small amounts of food and is able to do so all of the time. Susie's anorexia is most likely the _____ type.
   a. restricting
   b. bingeing
   c. maintaining
   d. maximal

4. As demonstrated by the woman in the second video, purging often leads to _____ for the bulimic.
   a. hysteria
   b. joy
   c. boredom
   d. relief

5. People with eating disorders typically
   a. think about food only at mealtimes.
   b. think about food more often in the morning than in the evening.
   c. think about food more in the evening than in the morning.
   d. think about food all of the time.

14.10 Borderline Personality Disorder

According to Erik Erikson's stage model, adolescence is a time when people develop a personal identity, their sense of self. For some people, finding a suitable identity is a fairly easy process. Others struggle to understand who they are and who they want to be. The important point is that some amount of intrapersonal turmoil is to be expected during adolescence. However, for some the struggle to find oneself is so severe that it becomes pathological. People who suffer from *borderline personality disorder* have little or no sense of self. They struggle to adapt in the world because they cannot predict their own behavior and often lose the ability to predict or understand how others will react to them. As you will learn from this activity, people with borderline personality disorder adopt a variety of behaviors to cope with their confusion about who they are. Virtually all of these behaviors are maladaptive, but because borderline personality disorder lacks the vivid psychotic behaviors associated with conditions such as schizophrenia, people often live with the disorder for years without seeking professional help.

TIP

- After watching each video clip, decide how ill you think Becky is. You can do this by jotting down a few words or rating her on your own ten-point scale; whatever method you choose, it should be is consistent. How did your evaluation of Becky change across the three videos? Why? Go back and rewatch the first video to see if you evaluate Becky's responses differently than you did initially.

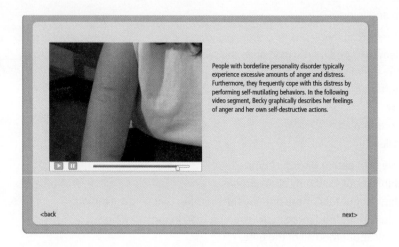

People with borderline personality disorder typically experience excessive amounts of anger and distress. Furthermore, they frequently cope with this distress by performing self-mutilating behaviors. In the following video segment, Becky graphically describes her feelings of anger and her own self-destructive actions.

<back   next>

REFLECTION QUESTION

People with personality disorders often have difficulties in relationships with others because they react in maladaptive ways to everyday situations. In the videos, Becky experiences several common occurrences but deals with them in ways that are destructive rather than adaptive. Recall Becky's description of her argument with her mother. How did Becky react? What would have been an adaptive reaction instead? Now recall Becky's way of dealing with a significant other who makes a rude comment toward her. How was her reaction maladaptive? What would have been a more appropriate reaction?

MULTIPLE-CHOICE ITEMS

1. A set of inflexible traits that prevents a person from functioning effectively within society is called a(n)
   a. mood disorder.
   b. anxiety disorder.
   c. psychotic disorder.
   d. personality disorder.

2. Which of the following is *not* a symptom of borderline personality disorder?
   a. reactive moods
   b. unstable self-image
   c. inability to make decisions on one's own
   d. volatile relationships

3. People with borderline personality disorder often rely heavily on their relationships with others to compensate for
   a. feelings of emptiness.
   b. delusions of grandeur.
   c. feelings of loneliness.
   d. a lack of conscience.

4. Often, people with borderline personality disorder will engage in _____ to deal with their excessive levels of anger or distress.
   a. social isolation
   b. self-destructive behaviors
   c. intensely creative activities
   d. vigorous exercise

5. People diagnosed with personality disorders
   a. have a secure sense of who they are.
   b. are usually hospitalized.
   c. rarely experience personal distress.
   d. often lead relatively normal lives.

14.11 Systematic Desensitization

Systematic desensitization is a method of treatment that has been successfully applied to overcoming phobias (see Activity 14.5) as well as other psychological disorders. Phobias are inappropriate manifestations of anxiety. The theory behind systematic desensitization is that a phobia can be overcome if the patient learns to control his or her anxiety about it. As you will see in this activity, the treatment involves training the patient to relax while slowly increasing exposure to the fear-inducing stimulus. Despite its effectiveness, some psychologists—particularly those who believe in Freud's theories—criticize systematic desensitization because it treats the symptoms of the phobia (anxiety) without addressing its cause. These psychologists believe that whatever is producing the original anxiety will soon manifest itself in a new way.

TIPS

- When you watch the video of the actual clinician, think about how the process of systematic desensitization differs in the real-world setting from the virtual experiment that you did with the rat. Is simply waiting for the patient's heart rate to reduce enough? What else does the therapist do to help his patient?

- Obviously, one big difference between the virtual experiment and real-world applications of systematic desensitization is the duration of the process. It can take months or even years for a phobia to be successfully treated using this method, but it is still a very effective method if both the subject and therapist are patient.

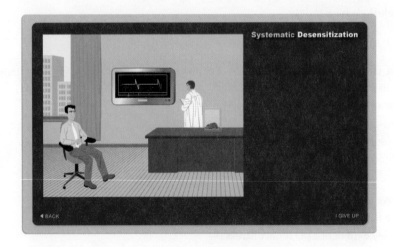

REFLECTION QUESTION

Jillian is terrified of speaking in front of people. Unfortunately, she has been assigned the task of giving an oral presentation to her introductory psychology class. How can you help her overcome her fear, using the techniques of systematic desensitization? Be sure to describe thoroughly each of the three components of the process.

MULTIPLE-CHOICE ITEMS

1. An irrational, persistent fear of an object, activity, or situation is called a(n)
   a. phobia.
   b. compulsion.
   c. obsession.
   d. reaction formation.

2. Systematic desensitization is based on what theory of learning?
   a. operant conditioning
   b. classical conditioning
   c. observational learning
   d. modeling

3. A typical anxiety hierarchy for a person afraid of flying might consist of
   a. a first step of taking the person on a plane trip while blindfolded.
   b. a first step of looking at pictures of a plane in a book.
   c. tensing and then relaxing the muscles of the face.
   d. deep breathing for several minutes at a time.

4. Systematic desensitization pairs
   a. anxiety-inducing stimuli with relaxation activities.
   b. a phobic person with a nonphobic person.
   c. positive reinforcement with negative reinforcement.
   d. real scenarios with imagined ones.

5. Research on systematic desensitization has demonstrated that
   a. it is not very effective in the treatment of phobias.
   b. it is quite effective in the treatment of phobias.
   c. it is much more effective with women than it is with men.
   d. it is much more effective with men than it is with women.

14.12 Compare and Contrast Approaches to Therapy

Diagnosing mental illness—even with the help of tools like the *DSM-IV-TR* (see Activity 14.2)—can be difficult, but once a disease has been identified, how does treatment proceed? As you might expect, there are a variety of approaches to treating psychological disorders. These variations reflect not just different techniques or different therapies but vastly different theoretical understandings of the origins of mental disease. This activity will present two individuals who suffer from obsessive-compulsive disorder (OCD). Then psychologists will describe the different therapeutic approaches that might be taken to treat a patient with OCD: behavioral, psychodynamic, medical, and cognitive.

TIPS

- As you listen to each of the major approaches for treating mental disorders, think about whether each one emphasizes treating the cause of the mental disorder or treating its symptoms.

- The end of the activity indicates that most modern therapists use a variety of approaches and try to tailor treatment to the individual patient and his or her symptoms. As you listen to each of the major approaches for treating mental disorders, think about which would be most effective with the two women presented at the beginning of the video.

You are a therapist who uses a variety of approaches when treating your clients. Twins Cadie and Sadie are seeking your assistance because both become extremely anxious whenever they have to meet new people. You decide to treat Cadie using a behavioral approach and Sadie using a psychoanalytic approach. Describe your treatment plan for each of these clients.

MULTIPLE-CHOICE ITEMS

1. Which approach to therapy focuses on the early stages of psychosexual development to provide insight into the causes of a person's disorder?
   a. behavioral
   b. psychoanalytic
   c. cognitive
   d. medical

2. Amelia often treats her depressed clients with drug therapy in hopes of adjusting the levels of serotonin in the brain. Amelia was most likely trained in the _____ perspective.
   a. behavioral
   b. psychoanalytic
   c. cognitive
   d. medical

3. Identifying irrational thoughts and challenging these thoughts is one goal of _____ therapists.
   a. behavioral
   b. psychoanalytic
   c. cognitive
   d. medical

4. Dr. Jones often uses the principles of learning theory when treating his clients. Dr. Jones is relying on which type of therapy?
   a. behavioral
   b. psychoanalytic
   c. cognitive
   d. medical

5. Which of the following statements is true regarding most therapists' approach to therapy?
   a. Therapists tend to rely most heavily on behavioral therapy when treating all types of disorders.
   b. Therapists find cognitive therapies to be highly ineffective.
   c. Therapists take an eclectic approach to therapy, relying on a variety of techniques from multiple orientations.
   d. Therapists unanimously agree that medical therapies are the most effective in treating psychological disorders.

Social Psychology

15.1 Fundamental Attribution Error

Most people don't like to admit that they lie, but everybody lies on occasion. And no matter how we might try to avoid it, we often get caught telling a lie. Think about the last time you were caught telling a lie to someone. Why did you lie? Did you lie to protect someone's feelings? to avoid getting in trouble? to get something you wanted? Did telling the lie lower your opinion of yourself? Does your lie indicate that you are *generally* not a trustworthy person?

Now think about the last time you learned that someone had lied to you. Why do you think that person lied? Was his or her motivation noble (to protect someone's feelings) or not (to avoid trouble)? More importantly, did learning about the lie lower your opinion of the person who lied to you? Does the person's lie indicate that she or he is *generally* not a trustworthy person?

People tend to explain their own behavior differently from the behavior of others. We view other people's behavior as being the result of stable, internal personality characteristics. We view our own behavior as being the result of external causes like the present situation. If someone lies to us, it is because they are a bad person. If we lie to someone else, it is because we found ourselves in a situation where a lie was our best option. This activity will try to demonstrate the fundamental attribution error by asking you to assess yourself, a good friend, and a public figure to determine whether you fall prey to this common judgment error.

TIPS

- When completing this task, be sure not to respond too quickly; think carefully about yourself, your friend, and the public figure before giving an answer.

- Use the response "Depends" if you have observed the person in question engage in different kinds of behaviors on different occasions (e.g., sometimes sincere, sometime insincere).

REFLECTION QUESTIONS

1. You ask an acquaintance, Shelly, to meet you at the library at 1:00 PM to study for a psychology exam, but Shelly never shows up. List both a dispositional and a situational reason for Shelly's behavior. Which reason is more likely generated by our tendency to apply the fundamental attribution error?

2. Have you ever been a victim of the fundamental attribution error? Describe the experience. What was the real cause of your behavior? What did the other person involved believe the cause to be?

MULTIPLE-CHOICE ITEMS

1. The tendency to over-attribute others' behavior to dispositional causes and underestimate the importance of a situation is called the
   a. halo effect.
   b. self-serving bias.
   c. fundamental attribution error.
   d. assumed similarity bias.

2. A stranger goes straight to the front of a long line waiting to speak with a customer-service representative at a department store. In applying the fundamental attribution error, you would most likely think that
   a. the stranger is a rude person.
   b. the stranger must have an emergency.
   c. the stranger didn't notice the line of other customers waiting.
   d. that stranger was told by another employee to go straight to the front of the line.

3. People are most likely to apply the fundamental attribution error to
   a. themselves.   c. a good friend.
   b. a parent.   d. a celebrity.

4. Samantha rushes into her dorm room and yells at her roommate for leaving a mess on Samantha's desk. Which of the following is a dispositional attribution for Samantha's behavior?
   a. Samantha learned in class earlier that day that she had received a low test score on an exam.
   b. Samantha's mother just yelled at her for leaving her wallet on the bus.
   c. Samantha is a person who is easily irritated.
   d. Samantha had just spent an hour cleaning up her desk.

5. We are most likely to apply the fundamental attribution error to _____ and least likely to apply it to _____
   a. a stranger; ourselves.   c. ourselves; a friend.
   b. ourselves; a stranger.   d. a friend; a stranger.

15.2 Prejudice

We are bombarded with an overwhelming array of information every day. Because we cannot possibly consider every stimulus we encounter in detail, we often use simple rules of thumb (see Activity 8.2, "Heuristics") to help us make quick decisions. We face a similar dilemma when we meet a new person. Can we trust a new coworker? Will we get along? Will this person be competent at the job? Carefully answering these questions would take a great deal of time and energy, more than we might typically have. So we often rely on *interpersonal heuristics* to help us make quick decisions. We form expectations about whether we will like other people based on how they wear their hair, the way they dress, or the kinds of music they like. Although the term *interpersonal heuristics* may sound harmless, what we are really talking about is stereotypes. Like any heuristics, stereotypes are prone to error. What makes stereotyping errors destructive is that they frequently lead us to treat people with less respect than they deserve or to deny people opportunities (e.g., jobs) that they have earned. In this activity, you will have an opportunity to experience how stereotypes influence the way people are judged.

TIPS

- Listen carefully to the two speakers, as you will be asked very detailed questions. Think about how well each of the speakers structures his argument, as well as the evidence each of them uses to support his claims.

- After you complete the activity, have a friend listen to the two speakers, but do not let them see the screen, and don't tell them the backgrounds of the two speakers. See how their responses compare to the ones you made. Did their responses show more or less evidence of prejudice than yours? Why?

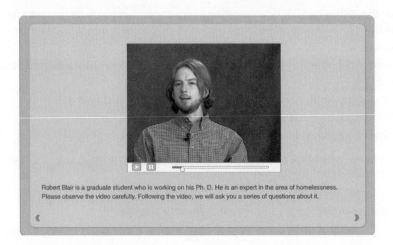

Robert Blair is a graduate student who is working on his Ph. D. He is an expert in the area of homelessness. Please observe the video carefully. Following the video, we will ask you a series of questions about it.

Think of a social group on campus (e.g., an athletic team, residents of a dorm, a political group, a fraternity or sorority). Are there commonly held stereotypes about this group? What are they? Why do you think these stereotypes developed? Can you think of a member of this group who does not fit the stereotype you described? Can you think of a behavior of this group that does not fit the stereotype you described? Does generating these examples alter your beliefs about this group in any ways?

MULTIPLE-CHOICE ITEMS

1. Stereotypes are
   a. generalized beliefs about particular social groups.
   b. positive or negative attitudes regarding a person based solely on his or her membership in a group.
   c. a negative or positive action toward a person based on his or her membership in a social group.
   d. All of the above

2. A danger of using stereotypes is that
   a. they often oversimplify the world.
   b. they cause us to view people not as individuals but rather as typical group members.
   c. Both a and b
   d. Neither a nor b

3. A common stereotype regarding people with mental illness is that
   a. they are well educated.
   b. they are highly successful.
   c. they are usually women.
   d. they are irrational.

4. Which of the following is a stereotype?
   a. Gunther promotes only Caucasians to high-ranking positions in his company.
   b. Megan believes that Tiffany (an African American female) must be a good athlete.
   c. Zoe chooses five females to work on her group project, even though there are eleven males and seven females in the class.
   d. Clarence feels quite uncomfortable around older people.

5. Which of the following is true regarding stereotypes?
   a. People form stereotypes only of disadvantaged groups.
   b. Stereotypes usually do not influence our attitudes.
   c. Stereotypes are more dangerous to groups with relatively low power in society.
   d. Stereotypes are basically harmless.

15.3 Social Cognition: Stereotype Threat

Group differences are observed on many kinds of standardized tests. Men tend to perform better than women on tests of math and quantitative reasoning. European American students tend to score higher than African American students on aptitude tests like the SAT. One question that is often raised about these group differences is whether they accurately reflect differences in ability (see Activity 8.4, "IQ Tests: Are they Accurate Measures of Intelligence?"). Are men really better at math than women, or do other factors contribute to the observed gender differences? If other factors influence performance, what are they? Dr. Calude Steele hypothesized that the stereotypes held about a group can influence performance by members of the group. For example, consider the commonly held stereotype that men are better than women at mathematics. According to Dr. Steele's hypothesis, when women are placed in a situation in which mathematical competence is to be tested, the knowledge of that stereotype can cause women to feel threatened, which in turn negatively influences their performance. The video you are about to see will describe the kinds of experiments Dr. Steele performed to obtain data consistent with his hypothesis.

TIPS

- Although the idea that stereotypes can negatively or positively influence behavior by a stereotyped group is largely accepted, researchers still are not entirely sure how stereotypes affect performance. As you watch the video, think about the mechanism by which stereotypes might influence mental performance.

- The following article provides an interesting account of how Dr. Steele initially developed and tested his stereotype threat theory: Steele, C. M. (2003). Through the back door to theory. *Psychological Inquiry*, 14, 314–17.

We all belong to groups that have negative stereotypes associated with them. Think of a negative stereotype that applies to you (based on your age, gender, race, sexual orientation, hobbies, etc.), and describe it. Have you ever been in a situation when you felt threatened by this stereotype? Do you think that your awareness of the stereotype in that situation hurt your performance in some way? Were you able to overcome the stereotype? If so, how did you do this? If not, why do you think it persists for you?

MULTIPLE-CHOICE ITEMS

1. Stereotype threat occurs when
   a. a person's performance is influenced by the threat of a stereotype.
   b. members of the majority group threaten members of a minority group.
   c. a person begins to believe negative stereotypes about others based on their group identification.
   d. a stereotype is created about a particular group.

2. Stereotype threat can potentially affect which of the following groups of people?
   a. Latin American high school students
   b. White middle-class males
   c. female senior citizens
   d. All of the above

3. In the experiment described in the video, the results demonstrated that
   a. black males outperformed white males on a test when it was described as measuring one's natural athletic ability.
   b. white males outperformed black males on a test when it was described as measuring one's sports-strategy intelligence.
   c. Both a and b
   d. Neither a nor b

4. Which of the following might be caused by stereotype threat?
   a. Billy, a white male, does poorly on a crossword puzzle.
   b. Elsa, a senior citizen, does very well on a memory test.
   c. Mike, a black male, does poorly on the SAT test.
   d. Susan, a black female, does very well on a math test.

5. Bridget, a female, knows that a negative stereotype exists regarding women and math performance. Stereotype threat suggests that
   a. Bridget will never do well in her math classes.
   b. if she is reminded of her gender prior to taking a math test, Bridget might perform worse than she would have otherwise.
   c. Bridget is likely to do better than most males on math tests in school.
   d. Bridget will not believe the negative stereotype regarding women and math.

15.4 Asch's Conformity Study

Fifty years ago, Solomon Asch conducted a pioneering study on social conformity. This video presents a modern replication of that earlier study to see if people today would still be likely to give responses that they almost certainly knew to be wrong in order to conform to the responses given by the group. Many people who watch videos or read descriptions about the Asch study claim that they would never respond the way the subjects in the experiment do; they say that they would give the correct answer regardless of how other people in the room responded. The question to ask yourself—if you believe this—is why? Why do you think you are different from the subjects in the experiment—both the modern version and the version conducted half a century ago? Why would you be more resistant to the influence of a social group than the subjects in this experiment? In actuality, you are probably not all that different from the subjects and your behavior would not be all that different either.

TIPS

- One important thing to note about the procedure is that the confederates initially give the right answer for a few trials. Do you think the same behaviors would be observed if the confederates always gave the wrong answer?

- As you watch the video, think about what other factors might have influenced the conformity of the subjects in an Asch experiment. For example, would the age or the gender of the confederates have made subjects more or less likely to conform? Why?

REFLECTION QUESTION

We have all conformed to group behavior at one time or another. We might do "the wave" at a football game or wear the latest trends in clothing. These examples of conformity are basically harmless. However, sometimes conformity can be harmful to oneself or others (e.g., vandalizing public property because all of your friends are doing it). Think of a time in your life when you conformed against your better judgment. Describe the experience. Did conforming make you feel better or worse?

MULTIPLE-CHOICE ITEMS

1. When a person goes along with the group, he is
   a. obeying.
   b. projecting.
   c. conforming.
   d. displacing.

2. In the experiment you viewed online, although seven people participated in the experiment,
   a. six of the participants were really confederates posing as subjects.
   b. the responses of the first three participants were not recorded.
   c. the female participants knew each other but the male participants were strangers.
   d. participants received payment for their participation only if their responses were 100 percent accurate.

3. The responses of the students appeared credible because
   a. they wrote down their responses first, then read them aloud.
   b. they were rewarded for each correct response.
   c. they were allowed to work in pairs before providing a response.
   d. they provided accurate answers for the first few trials.

4. Subjects in this study
   a. initially resisted the pressure of the group but eventually conformed at least once.
   b. never conformed to the incorrect responses of the group.
   c. always responded with the clearly incorrect answers if the other members of the group did.
   d. gave incorrect responses with a confident, happy demeanor.

5. The original Asch conformity study was conducted fifty years ago. Researchers who have run identical studies today found that
   a. participants were more likely to conform fifty years ago than today.
   b. participants were more likely to conform today than fifty years ago.
   c. participants were equally likely to conform fifty years ago and today.
   d. it was impossible to compare the two groups of participants.

15.5 Milgram's Obedience Study

Human history is littered with brutal campaigns of torture and murder committed by one political or religious group against another. These atrocities are not limited to the dusty old pages of history books. Over the last 100 years, we have witnessed the Holocaust, as well as genocidal campaigns in the former Yugoslavia, the Darfur region of Sudan, and many other places around the world. It is comforting to think that coordinated murder campaigns like the Holocaust can be blamed on a single monstrous individual like Adolf Hitler. But it is important to remember that although Hitler orchestrated the Holocaust, many individuals helped carry it out. Were all of the people who participated in the killing mentally ill? Could "regular," healthy, "good" people participate in these kinds of atrocities? This was the question on the mind of Stanley Milgram when he conducted his famous obedience studies in the 1960s. You may have a hard time believing how easy it was to convince regular, everyday citizens with no history of mental illness to inflict painful electric shocks on another person. Yet that is the legacy of the Milgram study: it would appear that we are all capable of harming others if an authority figure asks us to do so.

TIPS

- One thing the video does not make clear is that the buttons that the "teacher" used to shock the "learner" were clearly labeled. Many included labels like "Extreme Intensity" and even "Danger: Severe Shock." Even so, most of the subjects in the experiment administered every shock to the "learner," regardless of the label on the button or the response of the "learner."

- The Milgram study was conducted about fifty years ago, and many things about our society have changed in that time. In particular, people are more willing now to question authority than they used to be. As you watch the video, think about whether similar results would likely be obtained in current Western society. Why do you think the results would or would not change?

REFLECTION QUESTION

The Milgram study is one of the most controversial social psychological experiments ever conducted. Because of the psychological community's reaction to this study, the American Psychological Association created ethical guidelines that researchers must now follow when conducting their experiments (see Activity 2.6, "Ethical Dilemmas"). Why might this study be considered "unethical"? Do you think the knowledge gained from this study outweighs the ethical concerns?

MULTIPLE-CHOICE ITEMS

1. Milgram investigated obedience to authority based on his concerns regarding
   a. the Great Depression.
   b. the nuclear arms race.
   c. the civil rights movement.
   d. the Holocaust.

2. In the Milgram experiment,
   a. the "teacher" was the only actual participant in the experiment.
   b. the "teacher" and the "learner" were both participants in the study.
   c. the shock machine delivered only low-voltage shocks, regardless of the labels above each switch.
   d. the participants were recruited based on past experiences of harming other individuals.

3. Most of the participants in Milgram's study
   a. shocked the "learner" all the way to the end of the machine's scale.
   b. refused to continue to shock the "learner" after he stopped responding.
   c. did not participate in the experiment once they heard what was involved.
   d. gave a few shocks to the "learner" but never continued beyond the midpoint of the machine's scale.

4. Milgram's study demonstrated that
   a. people will give clearly incorrect answers to a problem when they believe the experiment is invalid.
   b. destructive obedience is rare; most people will not engage in it.
   c. people will obey commands to harm another person when they believe they are in a legitimate setting.
   d. people will quickly stand up to an authority figure when they are uncomfortable obeying that person's commands.

15.6 The Stanford Prison Study: How Power Corrupts

The Stanford prison study is another landmark study in the history of social psychology. Undergraduates at Stanford University were randomly assigned to play the role of either prisoner or prison guard at a mock prison in the basement of the psychology building. As you will see, the behavior of both groups of subjects was shocking and unpredictable based on their personalities and behaviors prior to the beginning of the experiment. The experiment demonstrated how the possession of authority—even authority that is established randomly by the flip of a coin, as it was here—irrevocably alters the way people interact with one another. Like the Milgram study (see Activity 15.5), this experiment demonstrates that our behavior is not determined solely by our personalities; environmental and contextual factors also play a role.

TIPS

- What do you think about the guard who was interviewed many years after the study? Does he strike you as someone prone to cruel behavior? Is it possible that participation in the experiment changed him?

- The Stanford prison study is frequently cited as one that could not be run today because of more stringent standards concerning the ethical treatment of subjects (see Activity 2.6, "Ethical Dilemmas"). As you watch the video, think about which aspects of the experiment might be considered unethical if it were conducted today.

- Think about the relationship between the Stanford prison study, Milgram's study, and Asch's work on social influence. Taken together, what do they tell us about human nature and our propensity to commit cruel and unlawful acts against one another?

REFLECTION QUESTION

The Stanford prison study was conducted using mostly White, middle-class males. Do you think the results would have differed using different subject groups? For instance, do you think that women would have reacted in the same manner? Why or why not? How do you think the experiment would have ended if males were the guards and females were the prisoners? What about the reverse? What about college students who grew up in dangerous neighborhoods? How do you think *you* would have reacted in each role?

MULTIPLE-CHOICE ITEMS

1. The college males who decided to participate in the Stanford prison study
   a. were allowed to select whether to become a prisoner or a guard.
   b. were given tests to determine if they would make a better prisoner or guard.
   c. were randomly assigned to be either a prisoner or a guard.
   d. were assigned as prisoner or guard and then reassigned to the other role halfway through the study.

2. Participants in this study typically
   a. adapted to their assigned roles very fast.
   b. were unable to portray their assigned roles accurately.
   c. had difficulty maintaining the appropriate roles for the duration of the study.
   d. were able to shift from the role of prisoner to the role of guard quite easily.

3. The students portraying guards became _____ rather quickly, while the students portraying prisoners became _____ rather quickly.
   a. cruel; submissive
   b. relaxed; anxious
   c. compassionate; entitled
   d. quiet; boisterous

4. The Stanford prison study ended after just six days (it was supposed to continue for two weeks) because
   a. the prisoners had successfully escaped the prison and quit the study.
   b. the guards became uncomfortable with their assigned roles.
   c. the conditions for the prisoners had become inhumane.
   d. a prisoner was killed in the experiment.

15.7 First Impressions and Attraction

Folk wisdom suggests that "you never get a second chance to make a first impression." This saying implies that it is very difficult to overcome an initial negative interaction with someone. This is why you are urged to be careful in how you dress and speak when going on either a job interview or a first date. Although psychological research often contradicts folk wisdom, this is a case in which the research supports a commonly held belief. Our judgments of other people are influenced more heavily by the first information we get about them than by any subsequent information we receive. This activity will give you an opportunity to experience the kinds of experiments that social psychologists have used to support the importance of first impressions. It should be noted that although first impressions are weighed very heavily, we frequently have opportunities to overcome a poor first impression. Job interviews and first dates may be extreme examples, because without a good first impression there is rarely an opportunity to present another side of oneself. Most of us can probably think of at least one current friend whom we did not particularly care for upon our initial meeting. So, although it is always better to make a good first impression, one should not be too discouraged if an initial encounter goes poorly.

TIPS

- Try not to listen to the personal descriptions more than once or twice when ranking the potential dating partners. The experiment is more likely to work if you don't overanalyze the descriptions.

- This would be another activity where it might be interesting to see whether your awareness of the purpose of the activity influenced your behavior. Read the personal descriptions to a friend, and have him or her rank each potential dating partner. Did your friend show the expected pattern more strongly than you did?

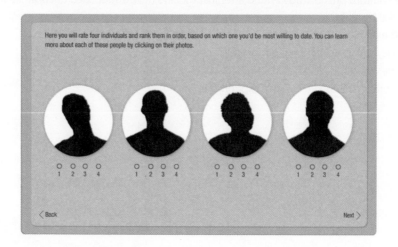

REFLECTION QUESTION

Have you ever made a bad first impression on another person? Describe the situation. Do you think the other person's perception of you in subsequent meetings was affected by this bad first impression? Were you able to rectify the bad first impression you made? Was it easy or difficult? Explain.

MULTIPLE-CHOICE ITEMS

1. In the United States, the biggest factor in determining interpersonal attraction to another is
   a. the similarity of the other to us.
   b. the number of times we interact with the other.
   c. how close we live or work to the other.
   d. the physical attractiveness of the other.

2. Jane and Blaine meet at a party, have a short conversation with each other, and then return to their friends. Later that evening, they have another brief conversation. In predicting whether these two individuals will be interpersonally attracted to each other, we should
   a. pay more attention to the first conversation.
   b. pay more attention to the last conversation.
   c. pay equal attention to both conversations.
   d. pay little attention to either conversation.

3. Janna describes Mike as smart, funny, selfish, and lazy. Vanna describes Ike as lazy, selfish, funny, and smart. Based on these descriptions, we are more likely to
   a. prefer Mike to Ike.
   b. prefer Ike to Mike.
   c. prefer Mike first, then prefer Ike.
   d. have no preference for Mike or Ike.

4. First impressions have a long-lasting effect on our perceptions of another person because
   a. they bias us for future interactions with that person.
   b. they create a context for us to subsequently assess a person.
   c. they are quite memorable.
   d. All of the above

15.8 Social Neuroscience: Using fMRI to Study Morality

Social neuroscience is an emerging approach to the study of behavior. As the name implies, social neuroscience applies some of the latest brain-imaging techniques to study questions that traditionally have been pursued by social psychologists. For example, modern society strongly discourages overt displays of prejudice. As a result, the fact that someone does not express prejudiced views does not mean that he or she does not hold prejudiced beliefs. A person may either choose to keep those views private or not even be aware of them (see Activity 10.1, "Gender Stereotypes: Implicit Associations Test"). Neuroimaging techniques could be applied to determine whether, for example, there is a conflict between one's stated beliefs and one's true beliefs. This kind of information would be difficult to obtain using traditional measures of prejudice. The article you will read is an example of social neuroscience. It uses fMRI to understand a persistent problem in moral reasoning: What determines whether it is morally justified to sacrifice one person to save a group of people? The authors propose that the answer may have something to do with whether people do or do not allow emotional reasoning to influence their judgments.

TIPS

- This is a fairly high level article, so do not be discouraged if you have to struggle to grasp some elements. In particular, the jargon in the results sections and the way the graphs are presented may be difficult for you to follow. If you pursue psychology further, you will learn how to interpret these aspects of research articles. For now, focus on the arguments that the authors make about the link between emotional reasoning and moral judgments.

- Brain areas are often referred to by the letters *BA* followed by numbers (e.g., BA 40); *BA* stands for Brodmann's Area, so *BA 40* refers to Brodmann's Area 40. This is simply a method of cataloging different regions of the brain. If you have not had any previous experience with neurobiology, this system will not make much sense to you. Again, do not let this distract you from following the authors' argument. For your purposes, the specific brain areas do not matter much. All you need to know is that whereas certain areas have been implicated in emotional reasoning, others have been linked to in more strategic thinking.

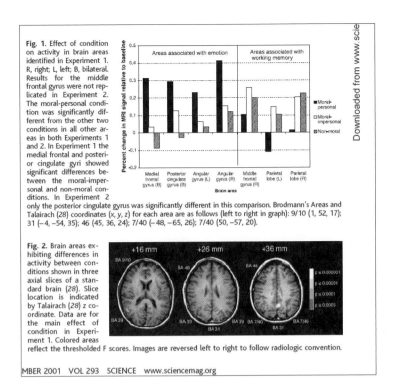

Fig. 1. Effect of condition on activity in brain areas identified in Experiment 1. R, right; L, left; B, bilateral. Results for the middle frontal gyrus were not replicated in Experiment 2. The moral-personal condition was significantly different from the other two conditions in all other areas in both Experiments 1 and 2. In Experiment 1 the medial frontal and posterior cingulate gyri showed significant differences between the moral-impersonal and non-moral conditions. In Experiment 2 only the posterior cingulate gyrus was significantly different in this comparison. Brodmann's Areas and Talairach (28) coordinates (x, y, z) for each area are as follows (left to right in graph): 9/10 (1, 52, 17); 31 (−4, −54, 35); 46 (45, 36, 24); 7/40 (−48, −65, 26); 7/40 (50, −57, 20).

Fig. 2. Brain areas exhibiting differences in activity between conditions shown in three axial slices of a standard brain (28). Slice location is indicated by Talairach (28) z coordinate. Data are for the main effect of condition in Experiment 1. Colored areas reflect the thresholded F scores. Images are reversed left to right to follow radiologic convention.

REFLECTION QUESTION

Although using neuropsychological tools to study human behavior has increasingly become the norm, some psychologists worry about relying too heavily on this approach. According to the skeptics, although behavior is produced by electrochemical activity in the brain, it is not synonymous with it. In other words, we cannot understand behavior simply by understanding what brain areas "light up" in an fMRI experiment (which is not to say that understanding brain circuitry is unimportant). How much do you think we can learn about complex behaviors like moral reasoning from studying fMRI or similar data?

MULTIPLE-CHOICE ITEMS

1. Greene et al. (2001) hypothesize that flipping a switch in the "trolley problem" is morally justifiable whereas pushing someone off a bridge in the footbridge problem is not, because the thought of
   a. flipping a switch produces relatively strong emotional reactions.
   b. pushing someone off a bridge produces relatively strong emotional reactions.
   c. flipping a switch eliminates any emotional reaction.
   d. pushing someone off a bridge eliminates any emotional reaction.

2. Given their hypothesis, Greene et al. (2001) predict that
   a. emotional centers in the brain will be more active when thinking about the trolley problem than the footbridge problem.
   b. emotional centers in the brain will be more active when thinking about the footbridge problem than the trolley problem.
   c. emotional centers in the brain will not be active during either problem.
   d. emotional centers will be equally active regardless of which problem a subject is thinking about.

3. In Experiment 2, the subjects who thought it would be appropriate to (for example) push someone off the foot bridge in the footbridge problem responded more slowly than those who thought this action was inappropriate. According to the authors, this difference in reaction-time data reflects the fact that
   a. the subjects were thinking harder about intellectual reasons to justify their choice.
   b. the subjects who considered this action appropriate probably did not understand the question being asked.
   c. the subjects who considered this action inappropriate probably did not understand the question being asked.
   d. the emotional reaction to pushing someone off the footbridge made it difficult for subjects to endorse this action as appropriate.

4. The authors concluded that the mental activity used to solve
   a. all moral dilemmas is more or less the same as the mental activity used to solve nonmoral dilemmas (e.g., deciding whether to travel by bus or train).
   b. all moral dilemmas is more or less the same, but the mental activity used to solve nonmoral dilemmas is different.
   c. moral dilemmas varies depending on whether the person is personally or impersonally involved in producing the negative outcome.
   d. moral dilemmas cannot be addressed productively using neuropsychological techniques.

5. The authors found the greatest amount of activity in emotional brain centers for
   a. nonmoral dilemmas.
   b. impersonal moral dilemmas.
   c. personal moral dilemmas.
   d. people staring at a blank computer screen.

I PSYCHOLOGICAL PERSPECTIVES

1.1 Multiple Causes of Behavior

1. c   2. a   3. a   4. d

1.2 Five Perspectives in Psychology

1. a   2. b   3. d   4. c   5. b

1.3 Subfields and Careers

1. d   2. b   3. c   4. a   5. b

2 SCIENCE AND METHODOLOGY

2.1 The Scientific Method

1. a   2. b   3. a   4. c   5. d

2.2 Naturalistic Observation

1. a   2. b   3. c   4. a   5. d

2.3 Self-Report Bias in Surveys

1. a   2. a   3. c   4. a

2.4 Correlation

1. b   2. a   3. d   4. c   5. d

**2.5 Designing an Experiment:
Dependent and Independent Variables**

1. b   2. c   3. c   4. b

2.6 Ethical Dilemmas

1. c   2. b   3. b   4. e   5. d

3 THE BRAIN AND BEHAVIOR

3.1 The Structure of Neurons

1. a   2. b   3. b   4. d   5. c   6. b

3.2 Areas and Functions of the Brain

1. c   2. a   3. d   4. c   5. d

3.3 Brain Lateralization

1. b   2. c   3. a   4. a   5. b

3.4 Localization of Function: Second-Language and Brain Plasticity

1. b   2. a   3. b   4. a   5. a

4   SENSATION AND PERCEPTION

4.1 Weber's Law

1. a   2. a   3. c   4. c   5. c

4.2 How Do We See?

1. b   2. c   3. d   4. b   5. d

4.3 Basic Sensory Processes

1. d   2. b   3. b   4. c   5. c

4.4 Perception: Integrating the Senses

1. d   2. c   3. a   4. b   5. d

4.5 Top-Down versus Bottom-Up Processing

1. a   2. a   3. a   4. b   5. d

4.6 Depth Perception

1. b   2. a   3. d   4. c   5. d

4.7 Visual Illusions

1. d   2. d   3. c   4. a

5   STATES OF CONSCIOUSNESS

5.1 REM Sleep: Thinking

1. a   2. b   3. b   4. c   5. c

5.2 REM Sleep: Dreaming

1. a   2. c   3. a   4. b   5. b

5.3 Drug Effects

1. a   2. d   3. a   4. c   5. b

5.4 Hypnosis

1. c   2. c   3. a   4. d   5. a

6 LEARNING

6.1 Classical Conditioning: Pavlov's Dogs

1. a   2. d   3. c   4. b   5. c

6.2 Classical Conditioning and Advertising

1. b   2. b   3. d   4. a   5. d

6.3 Operant Conditioning: Teaching a Dog New Tricks

1. a   2. b   3. c   4. b   5. d

6.4 Reinforcement and Punishment

1. c   2. b   3. d   4. c   5. d

6.5 Shaping

1. c   2. a   3. b   4. b   5. d

6.6 Schedules of Reinforcement

1. c   2. a   3. c   4. b   5. d

6.7 Observational Learning: Monkey See, Monkey Do

1. d   2. b   3. a   4. d   5. c

7 MEMORY

7.1 Sensory Memory

1. c   2. b   3. c   4. a   5. d

7.2 Working Memory: Decay versus Interference

1. c   2. b   3. d   4. a   5. d

7.3 Working Memory: Putting Memory to Work

1. a   2. b   3. d   4. c   5. b

7.4 Long-Term Memory

1. a   2. b   3. d   4. c   5. c

7.5 Levels of Processing: Transferring Information from Short-Term Memory to Long-Term Memory

1. a   2. b   3. a   4. d   5. b

7.6 Eyewitness Fallibility: Witnessing a Crime

1. a   2. b   3. c   4. d   5. c

7.7 Eyewitness Fallibility: Focusing Attention

1. a   2. a   3. b   4. c   5. d

7.8 Alzheimer's Disease

1. a   2. b   3. d   4. c   5. b

8 LANGUAGE, COGNITION, AND INTELLIGENCE

8.1 Thinking and Reasoning: Centenarians

1. c   2. d   3. c   4. c   5. d

8.2 Heuristics

1. c   2. c   3. d   4. b   5. a

8.3 Gardner's Theory of Multiple Intelligences

1. c   2. b   3. c   4. d   5. a

8.4 IQ Tests: Are They Accurate Measures of Intelligence?

1. c   2. b   3. c   4. d   5. a

8.5 Group Differences in IQ

1. d   2. c   3. a   4. c   5. d

8.6 Mental Retardation: Down Syndrome

1. b   2. d   3. b   4. d

8.7 Language Development

1. a   2. c   3. d

9 MOTIVATION AND EMOTION

9.1 The Need for Achievement

1. a   2. b   3. c   4. c   5. a   6. a

9.2 Emotion: Language of the Face

1. c   2. c   3. a   4. c   5. d

9.3 Emotion: Body Language

1. c   2. b   3. d   4. a   5. d

9.4 Detection of Deception

1. c   2. a   3. c   4. a   5. a

10 SEXUALITY AND GENDER

10.1 Gender Stereotypes: Implicit Associations Test

1. b   2. b   3. b   4. c   5. c

10.2 Sexual Response: Masters and Johnson

1. a   2. a   3. b   4. d   5. d

10.3 Sex and Medicine: Sex, Sin, and Sickness

1. a   2. b   3. c   4. c   5. d

10.4 Sex and Medicine: Alfred Kinsey

1. d   2. d   3. b   4. a   5. b

10.5 Biological Aspects of Sexuality: Sexual Identity

1. b   2. c   3. a   4. d

10.6 Adolescence: Sexual Identity

1. b   2. b   3. d   4. d

10.7 Sexual Response: Viagra

1. c   2. d   3. d   4. b   5. b

10.8 The Science of Sexuality: Evolutionary Psychology and Mate Selection

1. c   2. a   3. c   4. d   5. a

10.9 Adulthood: Interracial Relationships

1. d   2. a   3. b   4. b

11 DEVELOPMENT

11.1 Understanding Nature and Nurture

1. a   2. b   3. c   4. a   5. b

11.2 Genes and Behavior: Twin Studies

1. b   2. a   3. d   4. b   5. c

11.3 Infant Vision: Seeing through the Eyes of a Child

1. c   2. c   3. b   4. d   5. a

11.4 Cognitive Development: Categorization

1. b   2. d   3. d

11.5 Conservation

1. a 2. c 3. d 4. c 5. b

11.6 Stages of Moral Development

1. a 2. a 3. b 4. c 5. d

11.7 Adolescence: Adolescent Development

1. c 2. d 3. a 4. a 5. a

11.8 Suicide Risk Factors

1. c 2. a 3. b 4. d 5. d

12 PERSONALITY

12.1 Defense Mechanisms

1. d 2. a 3. a 4. c 5. c

12.2 Your Ideal Self

1. c 2. a 3. b 4. d 5. d

12.3 Trait Theory of Personality

1. c 2. b 3. b 4. d 5. a

12.4 Personality Assessment

1. b 2. c 3. a 4. d 5. d

13 HEALTH PSYCHOLOGY

13.1 College Stress Test

1. b 2. a 3. d 4. a 5. c

13.2 Type A Behavior

1. c 2. a 3. d 4. b 5. b

14 ABNORMAL PSYCHOLOGY: THERAPY AND TREATMENT

14.1 Distinguishing Abnormality: A Continuum View

1. c 2. c 3. d 4. b

14.2 Understanding the DSM

1. a 2. c 3. d 4. a 5. c

14.3 Depression

1. d   2. d   3. a   4. a   5. c

14.4 Bipolar Disorder

1. c   2. c   3. d   4. a   5. c

14.5 Phobia

1. a   2. b   3. b   4. c   5. a

14.6 Schizophrenia

1. a   2. d   3. b   4. a   5. d

14.7 Historical Perspectives: Treatment of Schizophrenia

1. c   2. d   3. c   4. a   5. a

14.8 Substance Abuse

1. d   2. c   3. a   4. b   5. a

14.9 Eating Disorders

1. c   2. a   3. a   4. d   5. d

14.10 Borderline Personality Disorder

1. d   2. c   3. a   4. b   5. d

14.11 Systematic Desensitization

1. a   2. b   3. b   4. a   5. b

14.12 Compare and Contrast Approaches to Therapy

1. b   2. d   3. c   4. a   5. c

15 SOCIAL PSYCHOLOGY

15.1 Fundamental Attribution Error

1. c   2. a   3. d   4. c   5. a

15.2 Prejudice

1. a   2. c   3. d   4. b   5. c

15.3 Social Cognition: Stereotype Threat

1. a   2. d   3. c   4. c   5. b

15.4 Asch's Conformity Study

1. c   2. a   3. d   4. a   5. c

15.5 Milgram's Obedience Study

1. d 2. a 3. a 4. c

15.6 The Stanford Prison Study: How Power Corrupts

1. c 2. a 3. a 4. c

15.7 First Impressions and Attraction

1. d 2. a 3. a 4. d

15.8 Social Neuroscience: Using fMRI to Study Morality

1. b 2. b 3. d 4. c 5. c